Puppet Plays Plus

Puppet Plays Plus

Using Stock Characters to Entertain and Teach Early Literacy

Laurel L. Iakovakis

Illustrations by Clarke L. Iakovakis

LIBRARIES
UNLIMITED
A Member of the Greenwood Publishing Group

Westport, Connecticut • London

Library of Congress Cataloging-in-Publication Data

Iakovakis, Laurel L.
  Puppet plays plus : using stock characters to entertain and teach early literacy / Laurel L. Iakovakis ;
illustrations by Clarke L. Iakovakis.
     p. cm.
 Includes bibliographical references and index.
 ISBN 978-1-59158-716-3 (alk. paper)
 1. Puppet plays, American. 2. Puppet theater in education. I. Title.
PN1980.I38 2009
372.67'4—dc22 2008028654

British Library Cataloguing in Publication Data is available.

Library of Congress Catalog Card Number: 2008028654
ISBN: 978-1-59158-716-3

First published in 2009

Libraries Unlimited, 88 Post Road West, Westport, CT 06881
A Member of the Greenwood Publishing Group, Inc.
www.lu.com

Printed in the United States of America

The paper used in this book complies with the
Permanent Paper Standard issued by the National
Information Standards Organization (Z39.48–1984).

10 9 8 7 6 5 4 3 2 1

Copyright Acknowledgments

Whitehurst, G.J. and Lonigan, C. (2001) Every Child Ready to Read® @ Your Library® is a program of the Public
Library Association and the Association for Library Service to Children, divisions of the American Library
Association. Every Child Ready to Read® @ Your Library® is a registered trademark and is used with permission.

In honor of my two fathers, Jack Landau and Constantine Iakovakis. They instilled in my sons a sense of humor, a hunger for knowledge, and a zest for life.

Contents

Acknowledgments

Special thanks to

My husband, Al Iakovakis, and my sons, Clarke and Ross, who support and encourage me every day

My son, Clarke Iakovakis, for his clever illustrations and for tirelessly helping me edit my work

My friend and fellow librarian, Jaclyn Pierce, who listened, laughed, and shared

My sister-in-law, Marcela Landau, who helped me with the Spanish

And the amazing staff of Douglas County Libraries, my friends and peers, who gave me opportunities to grow both personally and professionally.

Introduction

Presenting a storytime program can be one of the greatest joys in life. Children's librarians have an opportunity to share amazing picture books with an audience of people who have chosen to make storytime a part of their day. When I remember the number of people who bundled up the kids in the middle of a Colorado winter and loaded them into the car to come to my storytime, I can only feel honored.

With this pleasure comes a responsibility—the librarian must select exceptional children's literature for the read-alouds and enrich the experience with fingerplays, songs, and puppet shows. The Every Child Ready to Read® @ your library® Campaign presents librarians with the additional task of demonstrating to caregivers how they can foster the development of their child's early literacy skills.

Puppet Plays Plus helps you meet these main purposes of storytime:

- To entertain children and caregivers

- To boost children's interest in and enjoyment of literature

- To give children an effective early literacy lesson

- To show caregivers how they can incorporate early literacy lessons into interactions they have with their children.

As literature experts, librarians are already regarded as literacy coaches. These puppet shows are humorous scripts that enhance popular storytime themes, and each unit has been further enriched by adding accessible early literacy information for you to incorporate at storytime and for the parent to explore in greater depth at home.

The Six Early Literacy Skills

The Early Literacy Campaign is a joint initiative with the Public Library Association and the Association for Library Service to Children, divisions of the American Library Association. It is based on research by Dr. Grover (Russ) Whitehurst and Dr. Christopher Lonigan (2001). Further information about its history, Every Child Ready to Read® @ your library®, the Six Steps to Early Literacy, and emergent reading is available at www.ala.org/ala/alsc/ECRR/ECRRHomePage.htm. The prereading skills that children need before they can actually read, as developed by this initiative, are discussed below.

Print Motivation

Print motivation is an interest in books and literature. Storytime is a perfect setting for children to develop this skill. It helps children become motivated to learn to read because they have experienced that reading is fun. Children develop this skill through exposure to books and activities that involve reading. They learn that books are an adventure and will want to learn how to read on their own.

Vocabulary

Vocabulary involves language development. By learning the names of things and knowing how to describe them, children expand their vocabulary. Talking with children helps them to develop this skill, as does asking questions and allowing them to respond. When you add descriptive words to their responses, you are helping them learn new vocabulary. Pointing to objects and pictures in books and naming and describing what you see also contributes to vocabulary development. Revisit the new vocabulary words you have introduced in literature, songs, or puppet shows.

Phonological Awareness

Phonological awareness involves learning the sounds we use that make up our language. Sounds make syllables, syllables make words, words build sentences, and so forth. Word games, playing with the sound of words, rhyming, singing, and making up nonsense words help to develop the skills necessary to single out sounds. The ability to combine individual sounds eventually leads to sounding out words while reading.

Print Awareness

Print awareness develops as children become aware of printed words. As they come to understand that when you read to them, you are looking at the print on the page, they are developing print awareness. Bring this awareness to fruition by displaying words as part of the storytime room décor, by occasionally following print from left to right with your finger as you read, and by pointing to the written title of a book.

Letter Knowledge

As children become aware of language, they realize that each letter is different and that it has a distinctive shape, name, and sound. This is *letter knowledge*. Often children begin developing letter knowledge by focusing on the first letter in their names. You can show and name magnetic or die-cut letters as a part of your storytime literacy activity.

Narrative Skills

Storytelling is a *narrative skill*. When you make up a story or retell a story, you are using this skill. Puppet plays tell stories, so by using the scripts in this book, you are contributing to children's realization of this skill. Encourage parents to have their child retell stories from your storytime. A parent can also retell them to the child at bedtime or in the car on the way home.

Quick Reference

Print motivation:	Books are a fantastic adventure.
Vocabulary:	Learn new words.
Phonological awareness:	Sing! Rhyme! Play with the sounds of words.
Print awareness:	Words are everywhere.
Letter knowledge:	A, B, C—They all look different.
Narrative skills:	Tell me a story!

Meet the Characters

My appreciation of commedia dell'arte, an early form of Italian theater, formed the springboard for me to write my first puppet show. The basic idea behind commedia dell'arte is that the shows are based on recurring characters in familiar situations. The characters are exaggerated, and their behavior is predictable. This comic approach is perfect for the young audiences who attend library storytime. They enjoy the humor and come to "know" and like the puppet characters

Following this idea, I first developed a few stock puppet characters and then put them into situations that would fit into weekly storytime themes. In the scripts in this book you will meet seven recurring characters:

Piggy Rae has a deep southern accent. She won the Miss Pork Rind Beauty Contest in 2001. In the talent competition she sang (to the tune of Handel's "Hallelujah Chorus") "The Bellybutton Opera": "Bellybutton, bellybutton, bellybutton, bellybutton, bel-ly-but-ton." She is a way, way, way off Broadway actress and stars in Moosterpiece Theater presentations. She always appears on stage (unless otherwise indicated) wearing a pink feather boa. Pink is her favorite color.

Tommy Turtle is Piggy Rae's best friend and Bernie Bear's uncle. He is slow and cautious, lending others good, if unheeded, advice.

Mrs. Know-It-All speaks with a haughty British accent. (If you can't do a British accent, just use a haughty tone.) Her refrain is, "I'm Mrs. Know-It-All, and I know everything!" However, as you may suspect, she always gets it wrong. She has a TV show called *The Mrs. Know-It-All Game Show*. I use a big floppy fish puppet for Mrs. Know-It-All, but you can use any puppet of your choice for this character.

Alistair McMoose is the host of *Moosterpiece Theater*. He is sophisticated and intelligent and also speaks with a British accent. Because Moosterpiece Theater is way, way, way off Broadway, it is low budget and, according to Alistair, has "a silly plot, horrendous acting, and a completely ridiculous ending." He gets exasperated with Piggy Rae's ego.

Bernie Bear is a young boy who speaks as though he has a stuffy nose. He is excitable and mischievous. This character is in the same age range as the children in the audience and is the character with whom they most identify.

Granny is an elderly puppet and speaks in a high-pitched, warbled voice. She wears glasses (you can make some by forming craft wire into the shape of glasses) and doesn't hear very well. Usually she appears as Bernie Bear's grandmother. I use a grey possum puppet for Granny, but you can use any puppet that is white or grey to denote age.

Señorita Lana is the Spanish teacher. She is a white lamb puppet, because *lana* is the Spanish word for wool. To help teach some simple Spanish vocabulary words, this puppet interjects them into conversations. She is kind, patient, and soft spoken.

Other puppets: You will occasionally need additional puppets. Some are specifically referenced, such as a horse or rabbit. At other times you may use any puppet that you already have that has not been designated as one of the stock characters.

Special Features

This book offers ready-made scripts that enrich popular storytime themes. You can easily incorporate them into your storytimes and use the clearly described ideas to promote early literacy. The puppet plays are designed for presentation to ages preschool through grade 3, although with some creativity they can be adapted for older children as well. Each unit includes the following features:

- **Fully developed puppet scripts that may be performed by one person.** You'll enjoy performing these humorous scripts, which invite audience participation. They work perfectly as part of weekly storytime, special programs, and outreach. With minimal props and materials, they are easily taken "on the road" to preschools and day-care centers, where early literacy programs are always in demand.

  The limited set of characters and materials also means these skits are suitable for smaller libraries and those on tight budgets. Because the characters introduced in this book have names and personalities, your audience will remember them and begin to ask for them. Children look forward to puppet shows, and having characters that they know heightens their anticipation.

  Other features of the book have been added to minimize stress and help you use your time efficiently.

- **Complete list of materials needed, with a timeline.** For planning purposes, each unit contains a bulleted list of all materials needed for the performance. A timeline checklist is provided to ensure that on the day of performance you will have all the components in place.

  The props needed are easy to find. Complete instructions are given for how to create the homemade props used in some of the shows. It is assumed that you will have already designated a storytime area, with seating for children and caregivers, a low table and book stands for displays, as well as a puppet stage and puppets for the plays.

- **Suggested weekly storytime theme tie-ins.** For each of the scripts, several "related themes" are suggested. These are themes librarians often use for storytimes (e.g., manners, colors, grandparents). This allows for flexibility in how you use the scripts. By reserving one week for read-alouds and songs and fingerplays, and a second week for additional read-alouds and a puppet show, you can stretch your storytime theme to last for two weekly sessions.

- **Early literacy skill opportunities.** Each chapter offers tips on promoting early literacy skills during the program. By incorporating these literacy activities into your storytime, you will help parents understand how to talk about these skills at home. Also, keep in mind that as librarians we lead by example in modeling expressive, articulate read-aloud behavior. It is equally important that we talk about early literacy in a confident manner and model tangible examples of techniques that parents can use at home.

  The early literacy opportunities are designed to demonstrate to caregivers the various components that contribute to building literacy in children. These activities encourage the presenter to discuss an early literacy skill and give an example of what it means. This will help the audience understand the early literacy terminology. For example, "When you recite nursery rhymes to your child, you are building phonological awareness, which is awareness of the sounds that make up our language." Caregivers will come to understand the role they can play at home in helping their children build literacy skills.

- **Literacy To Go handout with booklist.** Each unit includes a reproducible letter to caregivers. It offers a tip about early literacy that ties in with the puppet show. The letter also contains an annotated bibliography of children's books suggested for checkout, so caregivers can use literature to pursue early literacy skill development at home. (Full bibliographic information for the titles, broken down by literacy skill, is provided in the appendix.) Place the Literacy To Go lists near the display table or hand them out after the program. Encourage caregivers and children to check out the books on display.

- **Promotional flyer to announce date, time, and location of puppet show.** To ensure your storytime's success, you must promote it in advance. Use any and all venues your library has to let library patrons know about the program—a newsletter, a Web site, e-mails, flyers, and so forth. A written invitation to attend the puppet show is included at the end of each chapter. Reproduce these and keep them at the children's desks, hand them to families as they visit, or add them to children's book bags at checkout.

  A goal of storytime is to boost children's interest in and enjoyment of literature. Advertising a puppet show performance increases attendance at storytime, and the children who attend storytime are learning that reading is fun—so spread the word!

- **Bibliographies of titles that connect with a literacy skill.** The bibliographies in the appendix are divided into early literacy skill sets. Use these lists to select titles for your early literacy displays and to support caregivers by featuring fun read-alouds that can help them segue into a literacy lesson with their child at home. Create an enticing display using a few props or decorations—suggestions are offered in each unit—or embellish the display with items that you already have on hand. This will encourage checkouts in a manner convenient for caregivers. Feel free to adapt your displays to highlight your library's collection.

  You may want to begin your own file of titles that lend themselves to developing specific early literacy skills. Continue to assess new literature in your normal manner—according to story line, illustration, and so forth—but also determine how you can use the book to reinforce early literacy skills.

Have Fun

Your personal enjoyment of your program is contagious. Practice the puppet show to ensure that you are confident in yourself and relaxed in your performance. Puppetry will add a new dimension to your storytime and your relationship with your patrons.

Patrons will come to identify you with the puppet characters. One afternoon I was in the library stacks assisting a teen patron with a research project. A little girl was in the library with her mother. She kept peeking around the bookshelves, staring at me, and then retreating. It seemed that every time I talked, she would stick her head around the corner. I waved; she stared at me. I smiled at her; she continued to stare at me. When I finished with my patron, I asked her if she wanted me to help her find a book. Her reply? "No. But you sound just like Piggy Rae!"

And I wasn't even wearing my pink feather boa!

References

www.ala.org/ala/alsc/ecrr/workshopsab/workshopmaterials/workshopmaterials.cfm

G. J. Whitehurst and C. Lonigan. 2001. Every Child Ready to Read® @ your library® is a program of the Public Library Association and the Association for Library Services to Children, divisions of the American Library Association. Every Child Ready to Read® @ your library® is a registered trademark and is used with permission.

PIGGY RAE
MEETS HER NEIGHBORS

Piggy Rae photo used with permission of www.puppetsathalfprice.com,
a division of The Book Fair, Inc.

Related Themes: Your neighborhood, Neighborhood helpers, Friends, Friendship

Overview: This show is perfect for programs based on themes of neighbors and friends. The early literacy skill focus of this puppet show is phonological awareness through rhyming verse. As Piggy Rae takes a walk in her neighborhood, she meets some important members of her community. Each neighborhood helper shares a rhyme about his or her job, and the audience repeats it.

Early Literacy Skill Focus: Rhyming words are one method of helping children discern the sounds that make up our language, which develops *phonological awareness*. You will also have opportunities to build *vocabulary* by talking about each character's occupation and the new words introduced in his or her verse.

The Literacy To Go sheet at the end of the chapter lists picture books with rhyming text. It also offers tips to caregivers about playing with verse at home.

Other Literacy Opportunities:

- **Vocabulary:** The show also includes vocabulary words that you will introduce to the audience. Talk about the occupations in greater detail than provided in the script by describing what neighborhood helpers do and the equipment they use.

  Start the conversation by asking, "What is a neighborhood helper?"

  Words such as *celebrity*, *tidy*, *extinguish*, *blaze*, *graze*, and *law-abiding* are also introduced. Talk about other words that are synonymous with them.

  - *Celebrity*, Famous person; superstar
  - *Tidy*, Clean; neat
  - *Extinguish*, Put out; smother
  - *Blaze*, Fire; flame
  - *Graze*, Eat; nibble
  - *Law-abiding*, Honest; trustworthy

- **Phonological awareness:** The Literacy To Go sheet features children's picture books written in rhyme. Rhymes are an effective way for children to develop their awareness of sounds. The rhymes in the puppet show, which are repeated by the audience, are a natural segue to the Literacy To Go display, which features books written in verse.

Materials Needed:

- Puppets: Piggy Rae (wearing her pink feather boa) and puppets of your choice to denote a firefighter, mail carrier, dry cleaner, and police officer.

- Badges or apparel, such as hats, to help designate the profession of each puppet (optional).

- No special props are needed for this program.

- Literacy To Go handouts for participants (see p. 12).

- Promotional flyers (see p. 14).

- Display books for checkout; use titles provided on the Literacy To Go handout.

- Display items that tie in with the neighborhood helper theme of your read-alouds: school supplies, toy police car, fire truck, mail, etc.

- Titles for read-alouds.

Preparation:

A few weeks or more before the program

- Decide on your program theme.
- Announce the storytime program in the library Web site and newsletter.
- Reproduce the promotional flyer (p. 14) and distribute copies to caregivers at the library.

A week or two before the program

- Select and gather several read-aloud titles that fit with your theme, as well as display books for checkout and puppets.

- Reproduce the Literacy To Go materials (see pp. 12–13).
- Practice the read-aloud books and the puppet play.

On the day of the program

- Create a display of checkout material based on the phonological awareness theme of rhyming verse.
- Decorate the table with items that tie in with the neighborhood helper theme for the display.

Puppet Show Performance Tips: If it is difficult to get your hand out of one puppet and into the next one, have Piggy Rae say something like, "Oh, I have to turn the corner here," or "Whoops! There's a detour ahead!" Then take her off the stage so you can use both hands to put on the next puppet.

She may then comment to the audience: "Are you still with me?" or "I'm glad I didn't lose you back there."

If you want to use a badge or hat to have your puppet look more like a police officer or fireman, feel free to embellish. Another option is to choose a puppet that can be associated with the profession, such as a Dalmatian as the firefighter puppet.

The Program

During the read-aloud segment: After welcoming the participants, gather the children and caregivers into a semicircle around your storytelling chair. Intersperse your read-alouds with some of the literacy activities described above.

Introduce the puppet show: Have the group assemble comfortably around the puppet stage. As leader, address the group with the following welcome.

> It's wonderful to have a storytime with great stories and at the same time learn things about our community. Today's puppet show welcomes you to Piggy Rae's neighborhood. She goes for a walk and meets some individuals who are important in creating a community. She thinks that because she is a famous way, way, way off Broadway actress, she is the most important person in the neighborhood. Perhaps she'll find out differently as she meets others.
>
> Each character says a rhyme to introduce his or her occupation. Listening to rhymes helps to isolate individual sounds that make up our language. This skill is called *phonological awareness*. The puppets will ask you to join in and repeat the rhymed verse. You and your child may repeat all or part of the phrases, whatever feels comfortable to you. Have fun with it!

Move to your place behind the puppet stage to begin the show.

After the puppet show: Bring Piggy Rae out with you at the end of the puppet show and have her say the last rhyme again, and have the audience repeat it.

"When I need some pepperoni,

I'll just use the te-le-phon-y."

Then have Piggy Rae praise the children for helping her understand the rhymes from the neighborhood helpers.

Encourage parents to check out the display titles and to pick up a copy of the Literacy To Go sheet.

Have the puppets tell the children good-bye.

PIGGY RAE MEETS HER NEIGHBORS

Puppets:

Piggy Rae (wearing her pink feather boa)

Puppets of your choice to denote the following characters:

- Firefighter
- Mail Carrier
- Dry Cleaner
- Police Officer

[Enter Piggy Rae.]

PIGGY RAE: Hi y'all! Hi, hi, hi! It is I, Piggy Rae. I decided to take a nice long walk around my neighborhood today. Because I am always so busy performing as a famous way, way, way off Broadway actress, most of my neighbors have not been lucky enough to meet me. I will walk around today and introduce myself. I am probably the most important individual in this neighborhood.

As I walk, I believe that I will sing the song that helped me to win the Miss Pork Rind Beauty Contest in 2001. [Sing "Bellybutton" to the tune of Handel's "Hallelujah Chorus."] Bellybutton, bellybutton, bellybutton, bellybutton, belly-but-ton.

Boys and girls, you can see why I am so famous. People come from all over the world to hear me sing. Oh look, here comes one of my neighbors.

[Firefighter enters]

PIGGY RAE: Hello, neighbor. My name is Piggy Rae. You have probably heard of me because I am a famous actress. Who are you?

FIREFIGHTER: I am Fred the Firefighter.

From *Puppet Plays Plus: Using Stock Characters to Entertain and Teach Early Literacy* by Laurel L. Iakovakis. Westport, CT: Libraries Unlimited. Copyright © 2009.

PIGGY RAE: A firefighter? I'm not sure I know what that is. When I was a little pig back on the farm, I used to mud wrestle with by brothers and sisters. Do you mud wrestle fires?

FIREFIGHTER: No, I don't mud wrestle fires. I extinguish fires.

PIGGY RAE: "Ex-tin-guish?" That is a big word. Boys and girls, can you say extinguish? Say it after me. "Ex-tin-guish"

[Audience repeats:] "Extinguish."

What does that mean?

FIREFIGHTER: It means that I put out fires. Listen to this:

I drive a red truck

With a big special hose

To put out a fire

Wherever it grows.

Anywhere there's a blaze—

If it's inside a house,

Or where cows go to graze,

I'll battle the flame,

'Cause Firefighter's my name.

PIGGY RAE: Oh my goodness! I'm not sure I understand. Can you say that poem one more time, please?

FIREFIGHTER: Yes. Let's ask the boys and girls to help us. Will all of you please repeat after me?

I drive a red truck

[Audience repeats:] " I drive a red truck"

With a big special hose

[Audience repeats:] "With a big special hose"

To put out a fire

[Audience repeats:] "To put out a fire"

Wherever it grows.

[Audience repeats:] "Wherever it grows"

5

Anywhere there's a blaze—

[Audience repeats:] "Anywhere there's a blaze"

If it's inside a house,

[Audience repeats:] "If it's inside a house,"

Or where cows go to graze,

[Audience repeats:] "Or where cows go to graze,"

I'll battle the flame,

[Audience repeats:] "I'll battle the flame,"

'Cause Firefighter's my name.

[Audience repeats:] " 'Cause Firefighter's my name."

PIGGY RAE: Oh my! I can see that it is important that we have firefighters in our neighborhood. You put out fires to save people's houses and property. You are a real hero! It was nice to meet you, Fred the Firefighter.

FIREFIGHTER: It was nice to meet you too, Piggy Rae. Have a pleasant walk!

[Firefighter exits.]

PIGGY RAE: My goodness. I think you have to be very brave to fight fires. Oh look, there another of my neighbors! I wonder what she does. Hi, neighbor, my name is Piggy Rae. Who are you?

[Enter Mail Carrier.]

MAIL CARRIER: I am Mildred the Mail Carrier.

PIGGY RAE: A mail carrier? Where do you carry it?

MAIL CARRIER: I carry it to your mailbox, of course.

I deliver the mail

All over town.

No matter the weather,

I'm always around.

PIGGY RAE: Can you tell me that one more time?

MAIL CARRIER: Let's ask our audience to help. Just repeat after me.

I deliver the mail

[Audience repeats:] "I deliver the mail."

All over town.

[Audience repeats:] "All over town."

No matter the weather,

[Audience repeats:] "No matter the weather,"

I'm always around.

[Audience repeats:] "I'm always around."

PIGGY RAE: So you are the nice lady who delivers all of my fan mail?

MAIL CARRIER: Yes, I am.

PIGGY RAE: And you deliver it even if it's raining?

MAIL CARRIER: Yes, even if it rains.

PIGGY RAE: Snows?

MAIL CARRIER: Even in a snowstorm.

PIGGY RAE: What about thunder?

MAIL CARRIER: No matter the weather, I'm always around.

PIGGY RAE: Well, I can see that you are a very important person in our neighborhood. My fans would be so disappointed if I did not receive their mail. As you know, my mailbox is stuffed full of letters from my fans.

MAIL CARRIER: You are a very popular celebrity, Piggy Rae.

PIGGY RAE: Celebrity? There's another big word! What is a "ce-le-brit-y?"

MAIL CARRIER: A celebrity is a superstar, like you!

PIGGY RAE: You're right! I'm a celebrity superstar! It all began when I won the Miss Pork Rind Beauty Contest in 2001. As you probably know, my talent was to sing the beautiful "Bellybutton Opera," which goes like this. [Sing to the tune of Handel's "Hallelujah Chorus."] Bellybutton, bellybutton, bellybutton, bellybutton, bel-ly-but-ton. I've had a world full of fans ever since!

MAIL CARRIER: Well, I could listen to you sing all day, but I must continue with my deliveries. It was certainly a pleasure to get to meet you in person, Piggy Rae!

[Mail Carrier exits.]

PIGGY RAE: [Calls after her.] Nice to meet you, too, Mildred! Hmmm, . . . I just met another important person in my neighborhood. I didn't know that there were others just as important as I am. Oh, look up there! I already know that lady! She is the dry cleaner. I will go to say hello.

[Dry Cleaner enters.]

PIGGY RAE: Hello, Doris, remember me? I am Piggy Rae. You help me keep my pink feather boa clean and fluffy.

DRY CLEANER: Of course I remember you, Piggy Rae. One day you spilled some pizza sauce on your pink feather boa, and you brought it into my shop to clean.

PIGGY RAE: That's right! You got the stain out, and I was tickled pink! Please tell all of our friends in the audience exactly what you do.

DRY CLEANER: It will be my pleasure.

Your dry cleaner knows

How to take care of clothes.

You'll look neat and tidy

From your head to your toes.

PIGGY RAE: That is so true. Let's say that together one more time.

DRY CLEANER: Your dry cleaner knows

[Audience repeats:] "Your dry cleaner knows"

How to take care of clothes.

[Audience repeats:] "How to take care of clothes."

You'll look neat and tidy

[Audience repeats:] "You'll look neat and tidy"

From your head to your toes.

[Audience repeats:] "From your head to your toes."]

PIGGY RAE: Doris saved my pink feather boa from disaster! I am too famous to be seen wearing a pink feather boa with a big ugly pizza stain on it! What would my fans think? Thank you, Doris, for being an important part of our neighborhood!

DRY CLEANER: Well, Piggy Rae, I better run. I've got stains to fight!

PIGGY RAE: Bye-bye, Doris.

[Dry Cleaner exits.]

PIGGY RAE: There goes another important neighbor. Look who else I see! I believe I see what they call a man in blue. It is a police officer. I will go say hello to him, too.

[Police Officer enters.]

PIGGY RAE: Hello there, Mr. Police Officer. My name is Piggy Rae.

POLICE OFFICER: Hi there, Piggy Rae. I am Paul the Policeman.

PIGGY RAE: I already know a lot about you, Officer Paul. Police officers are very important members of our neighborhood.

POLICE OFFICER: Indeed we are.

We keep our streets safe

And enforce all the laws.

We're proud to be called

Police Officers!

PIGGY RAE: Fortunately, I am a law-abiding pig.

POLICE OFFICER: Law-abiding means that you obey all the rules.

PIGGY RAE: I certainly do. I think that we should say your rhyme one more time, to honor the police. Will all of the boys and girls repeat after Officer Paul, please?

POLICE OFFICER: Thank you, Piggy Rae.

We keep our streets safe

[Audience repeats:] "We keep our streets safe"

And enforce all the laws.

[Audience repeats:] "And enforce all the laws."

We're proud to be called

[Audience repeats:] "We're proud to called"

Police Officers!

[Audience repeats:] "Police Officers!"

9

PIGGY RAE:	That was fun! I do love a good rhyme. Nice to meet you, Officer Paul. I thought that perhaps I, Piggy Rae, was the most important part of the neighborhood, but I'm happy to share the limelight. We are lucky that you are here to protect us. I have met so many important people in our neighborhood today.
POLICE OFFICER:	You're welcome, Piggy Rae. I'm proud of our citizens, too. We're all an important part of the neighborhood.
PIGGY RAE:	Well, I can see that now. Oh my goodness, what is that funny looking car up there with the big sign on its roof?
POLICE OFFICER:	Why, that looks like our pizza delivery person.
PIGGY RAE:	Okay, freeze! What did you say?
POLICE OFFICER:	Well, Piggy Rae, the folks in that house must have ordered a pizza for delivery.
PIGGY RAE:	I cannot be hearing right. Pizza delivery? Delivered—to your house?
POLICE OFFICER:	Why, sure! You just call the pizza restaurant on the phone, order your pizza, and they deliver it right to your house.
PIGGY RAE:	Oh be still, my beating heart. This is too good to be true. Are you absolutely certain?
POLICE OFFICER:	Of course. Some nights my family and I get pizza delivered to our home. Why, I bet everyone that you met in the neighborhood today has used pizza delivery before!
PIGGY RAE:	Did you know that pizza is my favorite food? I love pizza. Mr. Police Officer Paul, it was nice to meet you, but now I need to hurry home. I suddenly remembered an important telephone call that I need to make.
POLICE OFFICER:	Have a good day, Piggy Rae.
	[Police Officer exits.]
PIGGY RAE	Oh, I certainly will have a good day now. That walk in my neighborhood helped me work up a very big appetite. MMMMM . . . pizza! And it's delivered right to my house! I think I am about to meet the very, very, very most important person in my

neighborhood! The pizza delivery person is sure to become good friends with me! Oh, yum-m-m-m.

When I need some pepperoni,

I'll just use the te-le-phon-y.

Y'all, I'm sorry, but I gotta run! Bye-bye!

[Piggy Rae exits.]

The End

LITERACY TO GO

Dear Parents and Caregivers,

Many different occupations make up a community. When you talk about the puppet show at home, mention other occupations and how they contribute to your neighborhood.

The titles listed below are books that are written in rhyme. Listening to rhyme and making up rhymes helps build phonological awareness, which is knowledge of the sounds of our language. When children are ready to read, they will use this skill to sound out words. In the meantime, these books are enticing read-alouds.

See you next week!

Literacy To Go Take Home Menu

Books that build phonological awareness and feature rhyming text: Rhyming words and rhythmical verse help to build phonological awareness. Play with the rhyming verse as you read these books with your child.

Anderson, Peggy Perry. *Let's Clean Up!*
A frog tries to clean up his room, but it's not to Mother's satisfaction.

Dodds, Dayle Ann. *The Prince Won't Go to Bed!*
What will it take to get the prince to go to bed?

Edwards, David. *The Pen That Pa Built.*
Takes place on a farm in the 1800s. Celebrates farming and sheep-raising.

Falwell, Cathryn. *Scoot!*
While other pond animals glide and dash and splash, the turtles sit quietly—like stones.

Falwell, Cathryn. *Shape Capers.*
Learn your shapes and use your imagination to see what can be built from them.

Goldstone, Bruce. *The Beastly Feast.*
Hungry animals bring their favorite foods to a feast.

Greene, Rhonda Gowler. *This Is the Teacher.*
Written along the lines of "This is the house that Jack built," it is the story of a teacher's day and her active classroom.

Hindley, Judy. *Baby Talk.*
Rhyming verse follows baby's activities throughout the day.

Hubbell, Patricia. *Firefighters! Speeding! Spraying! Saving!*
A rhyming story about brave firefighters, with colorful pictures and vivid verse.

McHenry, E. B. *Has Anyone Seen Winnie and Jean?*
Two little dogs, Winnie and Jean, escape from their yard and have an adventure, with the police hot on their trail.

Mitton, Tony. *Down by the Cool of the Pool.*
This book will have you singing and clapping.

Postgate, Daniel. *Engelbert Sneem and His Dream Vacuum Machine.*
Engelbert uses his vacuum to suck up children's dreams and take them home to watch them himself. Imaginative.

Ryder, Joanne. *Won't You Be My Hugaroo?*
A comforting book all about hugs.

Sierra, Judy. *Preschool to the Rescue.*
Preschoolers help to rescue a police car, tow truck, and more.

Ward, Jennifer. *Over in the Garden.*
A garden bug version of *Over in the Meadow.*

Weeks, Sarah. *Bunny Fun.*
A bunny and mouse have a mischievous day.

Wilcox, Leah. *Waking Beauty.*
Sleeping Beauty is snoring. How is the prince to awaken her?

Wilson, Karma. *Frog in the Bog.*
A rhyming and counting book about a frog with a big appetite.

Wilson, Karma. *Moose Tracks!*
A messy house and a messy yard are easily explained. But who left the moose tracks?

Yolen, Jane. *Dimity Duck.*
Dimity Duck has a fun day with her friend, Frumity Frog.

You're Invited to a PUPPET SHOW!
Come to storytime and a special puppet show performance of

PIGGY RAE MEETS HER NEIGHBORS

Join the talented Piggy Rae as she takes a walk around her neighborhood and meets some important members of her community. She'll meet a police officer, a firefighter, and even the mail carrier who delivers her fan mail.

Our puppet show is specially designed for children ages three through eight and their parents, and will help build early literacy skills of phonological awareness by using rhyme and verse.

Date (and day of week): _____

At (library name & address, room number or area)

_____

PIGGY RAE AND THE BLUE RIBBON BLUES

Related Themes: Self-esteem, Farm animals, Fairs, Colors, Jokes, Puns

Overview: This versatile puppet play can be incorporated into a variety of thematic programs. The focus of the literacy activity for this storytime is vocabulary building, specifically through homonyms and homophones, that is, words that sound the same but have different meanings. The use of the word "blue" in the title of this show allows you to talk about what "winning a blue ribbon" means and what "feeling blue" means. Use blue ribbons as name tags for the children in the audience, to attach to the cover of the read-aloud books, and for the books on display.

In the puppet play, Piggy Rae goes to the state fair and meets animals who won blue ribbons. She begins to feel sad when she realizes that she is different from them.

15

Early Literacy Skill Focus: This show lends itself to learning about *vocabulary*, specifically homophones, homonyms, colors, and other new vocabulary words. Piggy Rae uses a number of puns throughout the show. You also may discuss that colors are tied in with feelings and expressions. The Literacy To Go sheet offers caregivers more tips on building vocabulary at home.

The rhyming verse reinforces *phonological awareness*. Each animal that Piggy Rae talks to shares a rhyme about why he or she won a blue ribbon. The audience is then invited to repeat the verse.

The use of name tags, as well as the words used on the blue ribbons attached to the books, bring the children's attention to the printed word, that is, *print awareness*.

Other Literacy Opportunities:

- **Vocabulary:** Building vocabulary by learning about homonyms and homophones is the skill supported by the Literacy To Go display and take home tips for this program. The puppet show features homophones, or words that sound alike but mean different things, such as "pear" and "pair" and "dear" and "deer."

  Before performing the puppet show, introduce the color blue and the term "feeling blue." For example, after the read-alouds or as the children are getting seated, you might ask them to point to blue objects in the room. With older children, you might ask if they have ever heard of "feeling blue" and ask what it means.

  After the puppet show you may talk about other colors that reflect feelings. For example, Piggy Rae feels jealous that all those animals won blue ribbons for things she doesn't have. She doesn't have a tail like a horse or floppy rabbit ears, so, she feels "green with envy." After Granny reminds Piggy Rae that she is special just the way she is, Piggy Rae feels glad; she is "in the pink."

  Idioms used in the puppet show include "hold your horses," "being sheepish," and "holy cow."

  The sheep's rhyme plays on two meanings of the word "cool": chilly temperature and hip personality.

  The phrase "skein of yarn" and the word "knitting" may also be new vocabulary words to the children. You may wish to bring a visual sample of each item to show the audience and reinforce the development of vocabulary.

- **Phonological awareness:** You will be emphasizing sounds throughout the skit by incorporating animal sounds into the lines—see performance tips below.

  Each blue ribbon animal shares a rhyme with Piggy Rae. Before the puppet show, talk about rhyming words. Ask what other words rhyme with "blue." Phonological awareness will be reinforced when the audience participates during the puppet show by repeating the rhyming verse.

  The rabbit puppet's rhyme is a limerick, which is a five-line verse with the rhyme scheme A, A, B, B, A. Older children may want to see the limerick and rhyme scheme written out on a display or a handout.

- **Print awareness:** As suggested above, you have attached blue ribbons to your read-aloud titles and written on the blue ribbon why you have given that book a blue ribbon—that is, "blue ribbon author," "blue ribbon story," "blue ribbon illustrations," etc. Follow along with your finger as you read what you wrote on the blue ribbon.

  As the children enter the room and write their names on the name tags, or as the parent writes the child's name, use one of the puppets from the puppet show to read the name.

Materials Needed:

- Puppets: Piggy Rae (wearing her pink feather boa), Horse, Sheep, Cow, Rabbit, Granny.

- Props: Skein of yarn, knitting needles.

- Blue ribbons—one for each child, one for each read-aloud, one for each of the puppets, and one for each selected title on the Literacy To Go display. These can be made using the pattern provided at the end of this chapter, be purchased, or be die-cut.

- Crayons and tape so the children can write their names on the name tags and stick them to their shirts as they enter the storytime space.

- Easel or wipe-off board, or printed handout with the words to the limerick that the rabbit recites (optional—for older children).

- Literacy To Go handouts for participants (see pp. 29–30).

- Promotional flyers (see p. 31).

- Display books for checkout; use titles provided on the Literacy To Go handout.

- Titles for read-alouds.

Preparation:

A few weeks or more before the program

- Decide on your program theme.
- Announce the storytime program in the library Web site and newsletter.
- Reproduce the promotional flyer (p. 31) and distribute copies to caregivers at the library.

A week or two before the program

- Select and gather several read-aloud titles, as well as display books for checkout and puppets.
- If using the limerick as a literacy opportunity, write the words on an easel or wipe-off board, or type and copy them.
- Reproduce the Literacy To Go materials (see pp. 29–30).
- Make or purchase the blue ribbons for books, puppets, and name tags for the children (see p. 32).
- Select titles from the Literacy To Go display that will have a blue ribbon. Make a note on each blue ribbon. For example, you may write "blue ribbon illustrations" or "blue ribbon author" to help bring attention to these books.
- Practice the read-aloud books and the puppet play.

On the day of the program

- Attach a blue ribbon to the books that you will be reading aloud and be prepared to share with your audience why you have given these books a blue ribbon.
- Attach a blue ribbon to the horse, sheep, cow, and rabbit puppets used in the puppet show.
- Create a display of checkout material based on the vocabulary literacy theme.
- Attach additional blue ribbons to the selected titles from the Literacy To Go display.

- Put up the easel or wipe-off board, if using it.
- Assemble blue ribbon name tags, crayons, and tape for the children to use as they enter the storytime space.

Puppet Show Performance Tips: Use sounds similar to those that the real animals make to accentuate the puppet's speech. For example, play up the long "A" sound in the words "tail," "braid," "parade," etc., to mimic the horse's neigh or whinny.

The sheep may make use of the vowel sounds that mimic the "baa" sound. Say "waaaarm" and "wooool," with a tremble or quivering sound in your voice.

Carry through with the same elongated vowels for the cow.

The rabbit speaks quickly and choppily. When you finish the lines that end with the "P" sound, make a popping sound two more times. For example, say hippity-hop (popping sound, popping sound).

Sometimes it is difficult to get your hand in the puppet while you are still working with a puppet on the stage. Feel free to add a line to excuse Piggy Rae from the stage, such as, "I'm going to go over to see that animal." Then you can use both hands to put on the next puppet.

The Program

During the read-aloud segment: After welcoming the participants, gather the children and their caregivers into a semicircle around your storytelling chair. Before each read-aloud, tell the audience what you wrote on the blue ribbon that you attached to the book. For example, say, "I'm going to read you this book because it has 'blue ribbon illustrations'." After reading a few books, introduce the literacy activities of your choice.

Introduce the puppet show: Have the group assemble comfortably around the puppet stage. As leader, address the group with the following welcome.

> I had fun reading stories to you today. Now I'm going to perform a puppet show that teaches a lesson about self-esteem and shows how everyone has something to be proud of. It is called "Piggy Rae and the Blue Ribbon Blues." Piggy Rae starts to feel blue, or sad, when she thinks that she cannot win a blue ribbon, or first place. Our show involves some wordplay and introduces some new words. The puppets will ask you to repeat some of the rhymed verses. This helps children learn about sounds. You and your child can chime in for the entire lines, or just the end words. Do whatever is most comfortable for you. OK, let's get started.

Move to your place behind the puppet stage to begin the show.

After the puppet show: Tell the children that they are "blue ribbon listeners" at storytime.

Show the children the knitting needles and the skein of yarn. Ask if they remember what they are. Reinforce the new vocabulary by repeating the words.

Talk about wordplay from the literacy skills suggested above that you did not discuss earlier, such as "hold your horses," "being sheepish," etc.

Tell parents that the display books contain other stories that use wordplay to build vocabulary. Encourage caregivers to check out these "blue ribbon display" titles.

Hand out copies of the Literacy To Go sheets to caregivers.

Have the puppets tell the children good-bye.

PIGGY RAE AND THE BLUE RIBBON BLUES

Puppets:

Piggy Rae (wearing her pink feather boa)

Horse, wearing blue ribbon

Sheep, wearing blue ribbon

Cow, wearing blue ribbon

Rabbit, wearing blue ribbon

Granny

Props:

Skein of yarn

Knitting needles

[Enter Piggy Rae.]

PIGGY RAE: Hi y'all! Hi, hi, hi. It is I, Piggy Rae. Famous way, way, way off Broadway actress. And, of course, winner of the Miss Pork Rind Beauty Contest in 2001. But of course you already know that since I am so famous and lovable.

You know what's fun to do? It's fun to get in your car and take a drive to the state fair. You get to see a lot of top-quality animals that people have raised, there's food, there's games to play, there's food, you can go on rides that make you plenty dizzy, and did I mention that there's tons of food?

Last year I ate so much popcorn that I had corn coming out of my ears. You might say that I had ears of corn! Ha, ha, ha! I just made a funny joke. You know, an ear of corn and I had ears of corn. Ha, ha, ha. Sometimes I think I should have tried for a career as a stand-up comedienne since I can be so funny. But, as fate would have it, I am a famous way, way, way off Broadway actress.

And today I'm taking the day off to go to the state fair. I want to see all the animals that have won blue ribbons. As a former beauty

From *Puppet Plays Plus: Using Stock Characters to Entertain and Teach Early Literacy* by Laurel L. Iakovakis. Westport, CT: Libraries Unlimited. Copyright © 2009.

queen, I know plenty about winning. When I was crowned Miss Pork Rind in 2001, I received a lovely tiara. It was beautiful and shiny and had hundreds of sparkly diamonds and rubies. I looked like the queen of England.

I'd like to invite y'all to come along with me to the state fair today. Together, we can admire the blue ribbon animals. Let's go!

[Exit Piggy Rae. Pause. Put horse puppet on other hand.]

[Enter Piggy Rae.]

PIGGY RAE: Well, here we are at the state fair.

[Enter horse puppet.]

PIGGY RAE: Hold your horses, folks. Look up yonder! I see a beautiful horse. Ha, ha, ha. That was another good joke. Hold your horses, I see a horse. I'm so funny! I just crack myself up.

[Piggy Rae gets near the horse.]

PIGGY RAE: Why hello there, Mr. Horse. My name is Piggy Rae. How did you win that blue ribbon that you're wearing?

HORSE: [Neighs.]

Yes of course,

I am a horse,

With a bright blue ribbon.

My long silky tail,

That's easy to bra-a-a-id,

Helps me to look special

When I'm in a para-a-a-ade.

PIGGY RAE: What did you say?

HORSE: [Addresses audience.] Can you help me tell Piggy Rae about my blue ribbon? Just repeat each line after me:

Yes of course,

[Audience repeats:] "Yes of course,"

I am a horse

[Audience repeats:] "I am a horse,"

With a bright blue ribbon.

[Audience repeats:] "With a bright blue ribbon."

My long silky tail,

[Audience repeats:] "My long silky tail,"

That's easy to bra-a-a-id,

[Audience repeats:] "That's easy to braid,"

Helps me to look special

[Audience repeats:] "Helps me to look special"

When I'm in a para-a-a-ade.

[Audience repeats:] "When I'm in a parade"]

PIGGY RAE: Oh, you mean you won a blue ribbon because you have such a beautiful long silky tail?

HORSE: That's one of the reasons.

PIGGY RAE: Oh y'all, he does have a long silky tail. I don't have a long silky tail. I only have a short curly tail.

HORSE: Yes, so I see.

PIGGY RAE: I'll never win a blue ribbon for a tail that you can braid!

HORSE: That's true.

[Horse exits.]

PIGGY RAE: Oh y'all, I wish I had a long silky tail. I feel sad.

[Enter sheep.]

PIGGY RAE: Oh, lookie over there! That animal does not have a long silky tail that looks good in a parade. I wonder why she won a blue ribbon.

SHEEP: Wool on a spool, rules! Baa, baa, baa.

PIGGY RAE: Is she bragging? I can see she's not at all sheepish. Ha, ha, ha! See, I made another hysterical joke. I said that the sheep wasn't sheepish. Oh, I'm so funny.

SHEEP: You don't need a brain to see that I make the best skein. Baa, baa, baa.

PIGGY RAE: I don't understand what that means. Why do you care about wool on spool? What is a skein, anyway?

SHEEP: You know, a skein of yarn! Wait here, I'll show you.

[Sheep exits, reenters with skein of yarn.]

SHEEP: Here is a skein of yarn!

PIGGY RAE: Oh, I get it now! I know what you do with a skein of yarn. Wait here, I'll be right back.

[Piggy Rae exits, reenters with knitting needles.]

PIGGY RAE: These are knitting needles. When I was living on the farm, Great, Great Granny Pig would knit snout warmers for all us little piglets to keep our noses warm on those cold winter nights. [Snort, snort.] Excuse me. Did you win a blue ribbon because you knit?

SHEEP: No, I grow the wool that is used for making snout warmers, scarves, mittens . . . .

PIGGY RAE: How do you grow wool? I grew some vegetables once in a garden. Do you have a wool garden? I want one, too.

SHEEP: You can't grow wool in a garden. I grow wool on my back.

PIGGY RAE: You mean instead of hair or fur, you grow wool?

SHEEP: That's right.

I won a blue ribbon

For my wa-a-a-rm, fuzzy woo-oo-l.

You may think wool is hot,

But I say that it's not,

Because to me, my soft woo-oo-l

Is entirely coo-oo-l!

PIGGY RAE: What? Y'all, I don't understand. She says she's cool when she's wearing wool???? Great, Great Granny Pig used wool to keep our snouts warm.

SHEEP: [Addresses audience.] Can you help Piggy Rae understand what I said? Just repeat after me:

I won a blue ribbon

[Audience repeats:] "I won blue ribbon"

For my wa-a-a-rm, fuzzy woo-oo-l.

[Audience repeats:] "For my warm fuzzy wool."

You may think wool is hot,

[Audience repeats:] "You may think wool is hot,"

But I say that it's not,

[Audience repeats:] "But I say that it's not,"

Because to me, my soft woo-oo-l

[Audience repeats:] "Because to me, my soft wool"

Is entirely coo-oo-l!

[Audience repeats:] "Is entirely cool!"

PIGGY RAE: Oh, now I get it. I want to be cool like you and grow wool on my hide. I can't have a wool garden, so I want to grow some on my back.

SHEEP: Only sheep have wool; pigs don't have wool.

[Sheep exits.]

PIGGY RAE: I wish I could grow wool. Ohhhh, I feel sad. I'll never get a blue ribbon for wool. All I have is a pink hide. Ohhhh.

[Enter cow.]

COW: Moo.

PIGGY RAE: Holy cow! Look at that blue ribbon. There I go again! More great jokes. I said "Holy cow" because I saw a cow. I have such a great sense of humor.

COW: Moo, moo.

PIGGY RAE: Who? Why it is I, Piggy Rae, famous way, way, way off Broadway actress and clever stand-up comedienne.

COW: Moo, moo.

PIGGY RAE: [Louder] I said it is I, Piggy Rae.

COW: Not who. Moo. Moo. Cows say moo.

PIGGY RAE: Oh, silly me. Cows say moo and pigs say [Snort, snort]. Excuse me. Did you get a blue ribbon for saying "Moo?"

COW: No, I got my blue ribbon because I make delicious fresh milk that is made into ice cream.

PIGGY RAE: I love milk. And it's good for you. It has lots of calcium for strong bones. See how strong my bones are.

[Cow touches her.]

COW: You do seem strong! Thanks to drinking my wholesome milk!

PIGGY RAE: That's right. Of course, I do like ice cream also. Strawberry is my favorite flavor. No, wait, I think I like chocolate best. Wait a second; maybe butter pecan is my favorite. No, hold on, I had some rocky road the other night that was over the moon!

Oh, there I go again! Ha, ha, ha. I'm talking to a cow and I tell her that her ice cream is over the moon. Remember that rhyme about the cow jumping over the moon? I'm so funny. There's just no stopping me.

So now, why did you win a blue ribbon?

COW: My milk makes the best ice cream.

Vanilla, cho-oo-oo-colate, whatever you dream.

It's a taste you'll ado-oo-oo-re,

So you'll eat mo-oo-oo-re and mo-oo-oo-re,

'Til your tummy

Is bursting with yummy.

PIGGY RAE: What? I didn't hear that. I got distracted when you started mentioning dreaming about vanilla and chocolate.

COW: [Addresses audience.] Can you help Piggy Rae hear what I said? Just repeat after me:

My milk makes the best ice cream.

[Audience repeats:] "My milk makes the best ice cream."

Vanilla, cho-oo-oo-colate, whatever you dream.

[Audience repeats:] "Vanilla, chocolate, whatever you dream."

It's a taste you'll ado-oo-oo-re,

[Audience repeats:] "It's a taste you'll adore,"

So you'll eat mo-oo-oo-re and mo-oo-oo-re,

[Audience repeats:] "So you'll eat more and more,"]

'Til your tummy

[Audience repeats:] " 'Til your tummy"

Is bursting with yummy.

[Audience repeats:] "Is bursting with yummy."]

PIGGY RAE: Have you ever heard of pig's milk ice cream?

COW: I cannot say that I have.

PIGGY RAE: Then I'll never win a blue ribbon for my ice cream.

COW: That's right. I don't think pigs win blue ribbons for their ice cream.

[Cow exits.]

PIGGY RAE: Oh, I do love ice cream, but I feel sad that I won't win a blue ribbon. I wish I could make blue ribbon ice cream. Ohhhh, I feel sad. I wish I had a long, silky tail and woolly coat, and flavorful ice cream so I could win a blue ribbon. [Cries.] Ohhhh, I feel sad.

[Rabbit hops up next to Piggy Rae.]

PIGGY RAE: Oh my, you startled me!

RABBIT: Were you crying? I can tickle you with my wiggly nose and make you giggle.

[Rabbit rubs her nose against Piggy Rae's nose.]

PIGGY RAE: [Giggles.] You're right! That tickles me. I was feeling sad because all these wonderful animals won blue ribbons, and I don't have any of the things that make them special. You are awfully cute. And look at that blue ribbon. Did you win because you're so cute and furry and you tickle people?

RABBIT: I am a rabbit named Mop-p-p.

My feet go hippity-hop-p-p.

I won best in show,

I'll have you to know,

For my ears that go flippity-flop-p-p.

PIGGY RAE: Hippity, flippity, what? I don't understand at all!

RABBIT: [Addresses audience.] Can you help Piggy Rae understand what I said? Just repeat after me.

I am a rabbit named Mop-p-p.

[Audience repeats:] "I am a rabbit named Mop."

My feet go hippity-hop-p-p.

[Audience repeats:] "My feet go hippity-hop."

I won best in show,

[Audience repeats:] "I won best in show,"

I'll have you to know,

[Audience repeats:] "I'll have you to know,"

For my ears that go flippity-flop-p-p.

[Audience repeats:] "For my ears that go flippity-flop."

PIGGY RAE: Oh, now I get it. You do have cute, floppy ears. And you've got four lucky rabbit's feet—I bet that's why you won. You've got a built-in good luck charm. There I go again, with all my funniness. She's a rabbit, so of course she has rabbit's feet, and I said they gave her good luck. Don't you think I'm clever and funny?

RABBIT: It's true that I have four lucky rabbit's feet built right in. I'm very proud of them, but mostly because of the way they help me jump. Do you want me to hop and you can watch my ears go flop?

PIGGY RAE: I certainly do.

[Rabbit hops and exits.]

PIGGY RAE: Look at that cute rabbit! She can go hippity-hop and make her ears go flippity-flop. I'm a pig, and I have short, pointy ears. And I can't hop. I'll never win a blue ribbon for floppy ears. I'm feeling very sad. [Cries.]

[Granny enters.]

GRANNY: Is that you crying over there, Piggy Rae?

PIGGY RAE: Whaaaa! Yes, it is I, Piggy Rae. Whaaaa!

GRANNY: Why are you crying? Are you lost?

PIGGY RAE: No, I'm sad.

GRANNY: Well let Granny give you a hug. That'll make you feel better. [They hug.] I'm here with Bernie Bear and his mommy and daddy. They are over on the big slide, having a blast. Do you want to come over and play with him? We'll share our picnic with you, too. If you are sad because you are lonely, then come and play with us.

PIGGY RAE: No, it's not that I'm lonely. I just met some beautiful animals who won blue ribbons. The horse won because he has a long silky tail. I don't have a long, silky tail. The sheep won because she has soft, warm wool. I don't have any wool.

The cow won because her milk makes the best ice cream. I have to buy my ice cream at the grocery store. And then I met a cute little bunny who won a blue ribbon for her ears that go flippity-flop. My ears don't flip or flop. Whaaaa, and that's why I'm sad.

GRANNY: But, Piggy Rae, you are special just the way you are.

PIGGY RAE: I am? But I'll never win a blue ribbon for any of those things.

GRANNY: Well, Granny's got some news for you. You win a blue ribbon for other reasons.

PIGGY RAE: I do?

GRANNY: Why, certainly. Tell me about your tail.

PIGGY RAE: I have a little curly tail.

GRANNY: And it's a blue ribbon tail, Piggy Rae. What about your skin? It's certainly not woolly . . . .

PIGGY RAE: No, it's pink!

GRANNY: And pink is your favorite color! And what about ice cream?

PIGGY RAE: Well, I can't make ice cream, but I sure can eat it . . . . I can eat it day and night!

GRANNY: And what about your ears?

PIGGY RAE: They are short and pointy, and they are pink, too!

GRANNY: You see what I mean? You are blue ribbon special just the way you are.

PIGGY RAE: Why, thank you, Granny. You always know how to make me feel better.

GRANNY: Okay now, you give Granny another hug [They hug.], and let's go over and say hi to Bernie Bear. He'll be so happy to see you and your curly tail and your short pointy ears and your overall pinkness.

PIGGY RAE: Are you saying that he'll be tickled pink to see me? Hey, I just made another funny joke! Oh, my! Look! I see an ice cream stand over there. Let's get Bernie and his mommy and daddy, and I'll buy everybody an ice cream cone!

And while y'all are all eating your cones, I believe that I'll entertain you with my new stand-up comedy routine. I'm a scream! There I go again! A scream, and y'all are eating ice cream. Move over Broadway! Make room for Piggy Rae, side-splitting good humor. Did I say "good humor"? Ha, ha, ha.

GRANNY: You're one of a kind! Let's go get Bernie.

[They exit.]

GRANNY: [calls from offstage] Bernie! Look who I found! Piggy Rae! And she's going to buy us all an ice cream!

The End

LITERACY TO GO

Dear Parents and Caregivers,

We enjoyed having you and your children attend our storytime today. Today's Literacy To Go tips and book suggestions involve vocabulary, specifically homonyms and homophones. These are words that sound alike but mean different things.

The puppet show's title, "Piggy Rae and the Blue Ribbon Blues," reflects two meanings of the word "blue." One is the color blue, and the other is an emotion. Talk with your child about other words that he or she knows that have more than one meaning, like "pear and pair" or "aunt and ant."

Go ahead, "get your feet wet!" Borrow some of the books listed below. You'll find that the text and/or titles of these books have words or phrases with secondary meanings. We don't want to "badger" you!

See you next week.

Literacy To Go Take Home Menu

Books that build vocabulary: These books introduce homonyms and homophones. Use the pictures in the books to talk with your child about words that sound the same but have different meanings.

Alda, Arlene. *Did You Say Pears?*
Stunning photographs pair homophonic words and phrases.

Barretta, Gene. *Dear Deer: A Book of Homophones.*
Aunt Ant writes a Dear Deer letter from the zoo.

Cazet, Denys. *Will You Read to Me?*
A cute story about a pig who likes poetry more than mud.

Cleary, Brian P. *How Much Can a Bare Bear Bear?: What are Homonyms and Homophones?*
Rhyming text introduces homonyms and homophones.

Couric, Katie. *The Blue Ribbon Day.*
There are many ways to win a blue ribbon.

Doudna, Kelly. *Do Not Squash the Squash, Line Up on the Line,* and *An Ear Is Not an Ear.*
Learn about the homonyms squash, line, and ear.

Feiffer, Kate. *Henry, the Dog with No Tail.*
Clever self-esteem story that also features a play on words.

Gwynne, Fred. *A Chocolate Moose for Dinner.*
Well illustrated book about popular phrases that can seem to have two meanings.

Hambleton, Laura. *Telling Tails: Fun with Homonyms.*
Fun! Silly pictures and text.

Howe, James. *Horace and Morris But Mostly Dolores.*
Makes vocabulary wordplay around various references to cheese.

Kasza, Keiko. *Badger's Fancy Meal.*
This badger badgers.

O'Malley, Kevin. *Gimme Cracked Corn and I Will Share.*
Every pun imaginable is used here. Very funny.

From *Puppet Plays Plus: Using Stock Characters to Entertain and Teach Early Literacy* by Laurel L. Iakovakis.
Westport, CT: Libraries Unlimited. Copyright © 2009.

Scheunemann, Pam. *Flour Does Not Flower, Fred Read the Red Book, Sam Has a Sundae on Sunday.*
> Learn the homophones flour/flower, read/red, and sundae/Sunday.

Thomas, Shelley Moore. *Take Care, Good Knight.*
> Dragons try to interpret a wizard's message, which has double meanings.

Walsh, Vivian. *Olive, the Other Reindeer.*
> Olive the dog thinks this popular song is written about her. Is she a dog or a reindeer?

West, Colin. *Buzz, Buzz, Buzz Went Bumblebee.*
> A bumblebee buzzes around all day until he finds someone who doesn't tell him to "buzz off!"

Ziefert, Harriet. *Night, Knight.*
> A lift-the-flap word comparative.

You're Invited to a PUPPET SHOW!
Come to storytime and a special puppet show performance of

PIGGY RAE AND THE BLUE RIBBON BLUES

This fun-filled show features our beloved Piggy Rae, who is excited to go the state fair until she meets the animals who won blue ribbons. Piggy Rae thinks that she'll never win a blue ribbon, and that makes her feel blue. What will cheer her up again, and put her in the pink? Join us to find out.

Our puppet show is specially designed for children ages three through eight and their parents, and will help build vocabulary, an important literacy skill.

Date (and day of week): _____

At (library name & address, room number or area)

_____

Be there or be square!

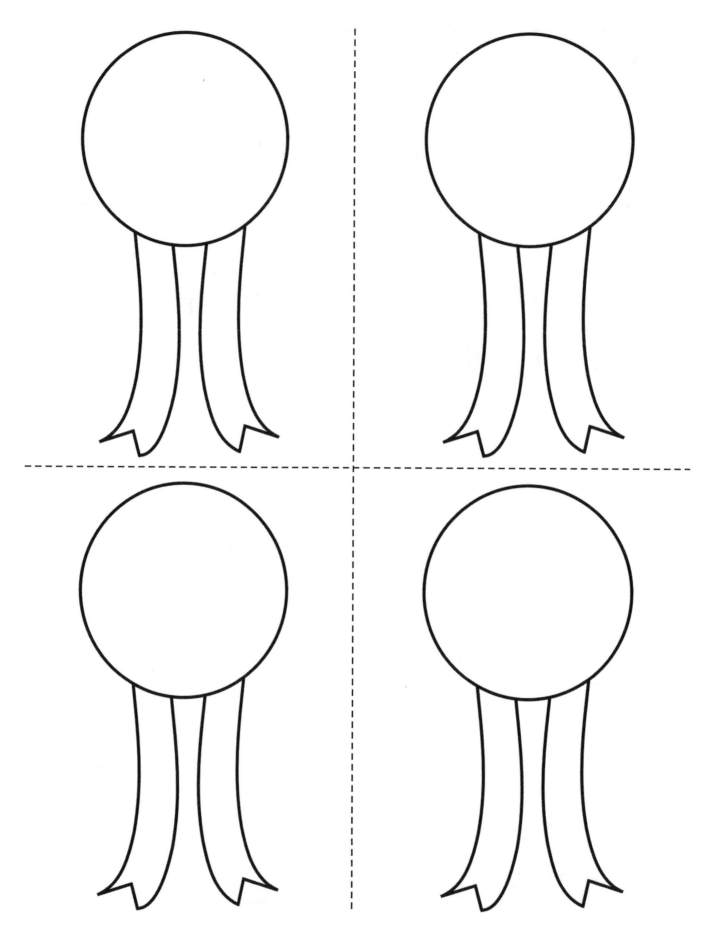

BEDTIME FOR BERNIE BEAR

Related Themes: Bedtime, Grandparents, Babysitting, Songs and singing

Overview: Singing, which is a learning tool of phonological awareness, is the focus of the early literacy skill used in this storytime program, which lends itself to a variety of themes, including bedtime, grandparents, and babysitting. In the puppet play, Granny is coming to babysit. It is Bernie Bear's bedtime, but he just can't get to sleep. He tries to induce sleep by singing lullabies.

Write the words to the songs on an easel or wipe-off board so the audience can sing along with Bernie Bear. Make teddy bear name tags for both the children who attend and the stuffed animals that they bring with them.

Early Literacy Skill Focus: The puppet show focuses on *phonological awareness* as the main early literacy skill, specifically with the lullabies and quiet-time songs sung throughout the show. Singing helps to break words into smaller parts, syllables, which are the building blocks of early literacy. The Literacy To Go sheet at the end of this chapter reinforces this skill; the booklist includes songs that have been illustrated and put into picture book format.

The puppet show also fosters the development of *print awareness*, in two ways:

- The name tags for the children and for the stuffed animals that you ask them to bring to storytime. Each child or the adult caregiver writes the child's name on one name tag and the name of the stuffed animal on another.

- Displaying the words to the lullabies that Bernie Bear sings reinforces the connection between print symbols and spoken words.

Other Literacy Opportunities:

- **Vocabulary:** New vocabulary words introduced in the text of this show include *varmints*, *swoon*, *sly*, *rascal*, and "counting sheep."

- **Phonological awareness:** Phonological awareness, specifically through the use of songs, is the feature of the Literacy To Go display and take-home tips. Before the puppet show, tell caregivers that singing to a child reinforces learning the individual sounds that make up our language. Suggest that they sing often with their children and not worry about perfect pitch. Encourage all participants to sing along at all of your storytime sessions. Then direct caregivers to the song lyrics written on the easel or wipe-off board, and sing together the songs that Bernie Bear sings in the puppet show. While singing, parents may wish to cuddle their children, who in turn may cuddle their stuffed animals. To model the behavior, you may hold the Bernie puppet, who may hold his small stuffed toy used in the puppet show.

- **Print awareness:** Before singing any songs, point out to the caregivers that you have written the words on the easel or wipe-off board, so they can join in singing with you. Tell the children that you have written the words to the songs. Follow along with your finger as you and the audience sing the lyrics.

  Talk to the children about the name tags. Each child has his or her own name written on a name tag. The name of his or her stuffed animal is also written out for people to read. Encourage parents to use the name tags at home to talk about letters of the alphabet.

- **Letter knowledge:** Show the audience the foam, die-cut, or magnetic letter "T." Tell them that it is the letter "T" and use it as a visual reinforcement of the activities suggested below.

  Refer to the easel or wipe-off board. After singing some songs, point out the "T" in "Twinkle, Twinkle, Little Star." Ask if any child has the letter "T" on his or her name tag. Ask whether anyone brought a teddy bear stuffed animal, which also begins with "T."

- **Narrative skills:** After the play, suggest that parents may wish to retell this story to their children at bedtime. This can be a joint endeavor, in which caregivers ask many questions, and together with the child, they remember the story. Telling stories reinforces the narrative skill. It also offers a parenting opportunity to talk about silly Bernie Bear and point out that we do not behave that way in our own houses.

Materials Needed:

- Puppets: Bernie Bear, Granny.

- Props: Baby blanket, small stuffed toy, plastic cup.

- Additional stuffed animals for children to borrow and for the Literacy To Go display.

- Teddy bear name tags, one for each child and one for each stuffed animal.

- Crayons and tape so the children can write their names on the name tags and stick them to their shirts.

- Foam, die-cut, or magnetic letter "T" to use for early literacy activity.

- Easel or wipe-off board with song words from the puppet show written out on it.

- Literacy To Go handouts for participants (see pp. 45–46).

- Promotional flyers (see p. 47).

- Display books for checkout; use titles provided on the Literacy To Go handout.
- Titles for read-alouds.

Preparation:

A few weeks or more before the program

- Decide on your program theme.
- Announce the storytime program in the library Web site and newsletter.
- Reproduce the promotional flyer (p. 47) and distribute copies to caregivers at the library.
- When you orally promote the puppet show, remind children to bring a stuffed animal with them to storytime the week of the puppet show. As the theme focuses on bedtime and bedtime rituals, the children will be encouraged to cuddle and sing to their stuffed animals as a part of the phonological awareness activity.

A week or two before the program

- Select and gather your read-aloud titles, along with display books for checkout, puppets, and props.
- Make the name tags. Use the name tag pattern provided (see p. 48) or a die-cut teddy bear pattern. You'll need one for each child and one for each stuffed animal.
- Name the additional stuffed animals that you have gathered for storytime. Write those names on name tags and attach them to the toys.
- Write the words to the songs on the easel or wipe-off board.
- Reproduce the Literacy To Go materials (see pp. 45–46).
- Remind patrons about the date of the puppet show and to bring a stuffed animal with them.
- Practice the read-aloud books and the puppet play.

On the day of the program

- Create a display of checkout material based on the phonological awareness theme of songs.
- Use the additional stuffed animals as a part of the Literacy To Go display.
- Put up the easel or wipe-off board with words to the songs.
- Provide teddy bear name tags, crayons, and tape for the children to use as they enter the storytime space. They need tags for their stuffed animals also.
- Acknowledge the names the children used for their stuffed animals. Point to each animal and say the name, following along with your finger. This helps to develop the print awareness literacy skill. Encourage caregivers to do the same. Or have the Bernie Bear puppet do this, as he can pretend that he knows the stuffed animals and greet them by name.

Puppet Show Performance Tips: Try not to let the props fall off the stage. Sometimes this can be challenging, as Bernie will be using his blanket and cuddly and needs to get a drink of water. During rehearsal, determine for yourself whether it is easier to leave the props on the stage throughout or to set them backstage and then retrieve them during the sequence of events.

This puppet show works very well if you play the pauses. Especially, allow for a quiet pause right before Bernie calls loudly to Granny, who is downstairs watching television. This usually gets a laugh. In addition, the audience enjoys watching Bernie try to get comfortable. Don't let the silence force you to rush the moment.

The Program

During the read-aloud segment: After welcoming participants, gather the children and caregivers into a semicircle around your storytelling chair. Intersperse your thematic read-alouds with some of the literacy activities described above. Read a story, then refer to the easel or wipe-off board to have the audience join you in singing a song from the puppet show, incorporating a literacy activity. Follow with another story. The puppet show will be most effective if you and your group have sung each of the songs prior to beginning the puppet show.

Introduce the puppet show: Have the group assemble comfortably around the puppet stage. As leader, address the group with the following welcome.

> I hope you all enjoyed our stories today. We have a puppet show for you that is all about getting sleepy. It is called "Bedtime for Bernie Bear." Granny is coming to Bernie Bear's house to babysit. It's already bedtime, and Bernie is trying everything to fall asleep. Please help Bernie get sleepy by singing lullabies with him. These are the songs that are written on the easel or wipe-off board that we have already practiced today. When it's time to sing, Bernie Bear will let you know. Please sing along with us!

Move to your place behind the puppet stage to begin the show.

After the puppet show: Encourage caregivers to check out the display titles and pick up a copy of the Literacy To Go sheet.

Let parents know that they can retell this story at bedtime. This also gives them an opportunity to talk about Bernie Bear's behavior; for example, "Bernie Bear was funny, but we don't behave this way at home!"

Tell the children that you enjoyed meeting their stuffed animals.

Hold up the letter "T" and have Bernie Bear say, "I know one more word that starts with the letter 'T'. It means good-bye. 'Ta-Ta!' Ta-Ta everyone! See you next week!"

BEDTIME FOR BERNIE BEAR

Puppets:

    Bernie Bear

    Granny

Props:

    Baby blanket

    Small stuffed toy

    Plastic cup

[Enter Bernie Bear.]

BERNIE BEAR: OOOOOHHHHH BOY! My granny's gonna babysit, my granny's gonna babysit! I'm so excited! I can hardly wait! My mom and my dad are going out, and my granny's gonna babysit!!!! I can't wait! I can't wait! I wonder where she is. [Pause.] I wonder what is taking her soooo long to get here. I hope she didn't forget!

GRANNY: Yoo-hoo!

BERNIE BEAR: OHHHH goody! That must be my granny! Granny! Is that you? I'm upstairs!

GRANNY: [Calls from offstage.] Hi, Bernie! Yes, it's your Granny! Come and say good-bye to your mommy and daddy.

BERNIE BEAR: Okay. [He exits.]

    [Offstage] Bye, Mom! Bye, Dad! See you in the morning! Granny, hurry up! Follow me upstairs.

    [Bernie reenters.]

From *Puppet Plays Plus: Using Stock Characters to Entertain and Teach Early Literacy* by Laurel L. Iakovakis. Westport, CT: Libraries Unlimited. Copyright © 2009.

Oh, boy! We're gonna have so much fun. We'll play checkers, we'll read some books, we'll watch TV, and I'll stay up really, really, really late! I can hardly wait!

GRANNY: Hello, Bernie dear. Come and give your granny a kiss.

[They hug and make kissing sounds.]

GRANNY: Now, did you wash your face?

BERNIE BEAR: Yep!

GRANNY: Good boy! Did you pick up all your toys?

BERNIE BEAR: Yep!

GRANNY: Good boy! Did you brush your teeth?

BERNIE BEAR: Yep!

GRANNY: Good boy! Well, then I guess it's time for you to go to bed.

BERNIE BEAR: What? I thought we would play some games and watch TV. And I thought I could stay up really, really, really late! My mom and dad always let me stay up really, really, really late.

GRANNY: Now, Bernie, your mom and dad said that it was time for you to go to bed. So I'll give you a kiss, and you go to sleep.

[They make a kissing sound.]

BERNIE BEAR: Oh, well, okay. I'm not really sleepy, but I'll try. Goodnight, Granny.

GRANNY: Goodnight, Bernie. [She exits.]

BERNIE BEAR: [Trying to get comfortable.] Oh, I don't want to go to sleep. I want to play. I'm not sleepy. But Granny said I should sleep. I'm gonna try.... Okay, now I'm gonna go to sleep.... Okay, here goes....

[During all of this, Bernie keeps rolling from side to side in lying down position, like he's trying to get comfortable in bed.]

I know, I'll sing myself a lullaby. I like "Twinkle, Twinkle, Little Star." Twinkle starts with the letter "T." Just like teddy bear, tree, and television. I wish I was watching television instead of trying to go to sleep. [Sits up and looks at the audience.]

Boys and girls, will you help me get sleepy and sing "Twinkle, Twinkle, Little Star" with me, please? First, I'll lie down and get real comfortable. Okay, let's sing . . . . [He sings with audience.]

> Twinkle, twinkle, little star,
>
> How I wonder what you are.
>
> Up above the world so high,
>
> Like a diamond in the sky.
>
> Twinkle, twinkle, little star,
>
> How I wonder what you are.

I always imagine lying in the grass and looking up at the sky when I sing "Twinkle Twinkle, Little Star." Let's sing it again and pretend that we're looking at the nighttime sky.

> Twinkle, twinkle, little star,
>
> How I wonder what you are.
>
> Up above the world so high,
>
> Like a diamond in the sky.
>
> Twinkle, twinkle, little star,
>
> How I wonder what you are.

You sing very pretty, but that reminded me of something. . . . [Pause, then he yells very loudly.]

GRANNY!!!!!! GRANNY!!!!! GRANNY!!!!!!

GRANNY: [Enters quickly.] What? [Out of breath.] What's wrong Bernie? What?

BERNIE BEAR: I need my blankie.

GRANNY: Your blankie? Oh, that's right. I forgot to give you your blankie. You startled me when you called my name and nearly gave me a heart attack! I think you left your blankie downstairs. I'll go get it.

[Mutters to herself as she exits.] That little rascal.

[She reenters with a small baby blanket.]

Okay, now I'll cover you, and you go to sleep. Night-night, Bernie.

[She tucks him in, they make kiss sounds, and she exits.]

BERNIE BEAR: Okay. That's much better now. Now I can go to sleep. I have my blankie, I had my lullaby, and I'm gonna go to sleep. [Rolls around.] Okay, now I'm gonna go to sleep. I need to get comfortable. Maybe if I try this . . . . [He stands on his head.]

Ouch! No, that was not comfortable at all. I should try another quiet time song.

Boys and girls, will you help me sing another song? Let's sing "Little Bo-Peep."

> Little Bo-Peep has lost her sheep,
>
> And doesn't know where to find them.
>
> Leave them alone and they will come home,
>
> Wagging their tails behind them.

That was nice, let's sing it again.

> Little Bo-Peep has lost her sheep,
>
> And doesn't know where to find them.
>
> Leave them alone and they will come home,
>
> Wagging their tails behind them.

That was a calm song, but . . . . [Pause, then he yells very loudly.] GRANNY!!!!! GRANNY!!!!! GRANNY!!!!!!

GRANNY: [Enters.] What! What's wrong now, Bernie? [Pant, pant, . . .] You're going to wear out your old granny.

BERNIE BEAR: I need my cuddly.

GRANNY: Oh. You need your cuddly. Where did you leave it?

BERNIE BEAR: I think that it is in the bathroom.

GRANNY: Okay, I'll go look, but when I come back, you have to go to sleep. Mommy and Daddy said it was your bedtime. Besides, Granny is watching a John Wayne movie. There are some varmints afoot, and John Wayne needs to take care of them, if you know what I mean. John Wayne movies make me swoon.

BERNIE BEAR: Maybe I could come downstairs and watch the John Wayne movie with you. I might like to swoon.

GRANNY: Oh, Bernie, you are a sly little bear. I'm sorry, but you can't come watch TV with me tonight. I'll go look for your cuddly now, and then you need to go to sleep.

[She exits and re-enters with cuddly.]

Here it is. Here's your little cuddly. Okay now, night-night, Bernie.

[They make kissing sounds and Granny exits]

BERNIE BEAR: Now I have my blankie and I have my cuddly, I'll sing another quiet time song, and then I can go to sleep . . . .

[To audience.] Will you all help me sing "Baa, Baa, Black Sheep," please?

> Baa, baa, black sheep, have you any wool?
>
> Yes, sir, yes, sir, three bags full.
>
> One for my master, one for my dame,
>
> And one for the little boy who lives down the lane.

I'm still awake. That didn't work. Let's sing it together once more.

> Baa, baa, black sheep, have you any wool?
>
> Yes, sir, yes, sir, three bags full.
>
> One for my master, one for my dame,
>
> And one for the little boy who lives down the lane.

Hmmm, . . . I have another idea. Maybe I should try counting sheep. I heard that works! You pretend to see some sheep in a field or jumping over a fence, and you count them until you fall asleep. I know how to count to ten.

Can all of you help me count to 10?

Okay, let's count. 1, 2, 3, 4, 5, 6, 7, 8, 9, 10.

That didn't make me sleepy at all. I know, I'll count backward, and when I reach zero, I'll be asleep. 10, 9, 8, 7, 6, 5, 4, 3, 2, 1, 0.

[He begins to snore immediately. Snore, snore, snore, . . . pause. He sits up quickly and speaks to audience.]

BERNIE BEAR: Ha, ha! Fooled you! Ha, ha, ha! [In a sing-songy voice.] I'm not asleep! Ha, ha, ha, ha, ha. That was funny. But all of that singing and counting made me thirsty.

[Pause, then Bernie yells very loudly.]
GRANNY!!!!!!! GRANNY!!!!! GRANNY!!!!!!

GRANNY: [Enters] What is it now? You have your blankie and you have your cuddly . . . . [Pant, pant, . . .] You're wearing me out. I'm going to be so tired from running up and down these stairs that I'm going to fall asleep and miss the end of my John Wayne movie.

BERNIE BEAR: I'm thirsty.

GRANNY: I should have guessed.

BERNIE BEAR: May I have a glass of water, please?

GRANNY: Well, you're a little bit naughty about bedtime, but you certainly have nice manners. Okay, I'll get you the water, but then you absolutely, positively, must, must, MUST go to sleep.

BERNIE BEAR: Okie-dokie.
[Granny exits and returns with a cup and helps Bernie get a drink.]

BERNIE BEAR: [Glug, glug, glug] Thank you, Granny.

GRANNY: Now, off to dreamland. Night-night.

BERNIE BEAR: Granny, wait! Now I need to tinkle.

GRANNY: I should have guessed that, too! Okay, let's go.
[They exit, pause, reenter.]

GRANNY: Okay now, Bernie. You've got your blankie.

BERNIE BEAR: Yep.

GRANNY: You've got your cuddly.

BERNIE BEAR: Yep.

GRANNY: You had a drink of water.

BERNIE BEAR: Yep.

GRANNY: You went potty.

BERNIE BEAR: Yep.

GRANNY: Anything else that you can think of?

BERNIE BEAR: Nope.

GRANNY: Then give me a kiss good-night.

[They make kissing sounds and Granny exits]

BERNIE BEAR: [Still trying to get comfortable.] Well, that's it. Now I can go to sleep… . Come on dreams . . . . Dreams! Where are you? I'm waiting . . . . Hmm, this isn't working. [Sings to tune of "Rock-a-Bye-Baby":] Nighty-night, sleepy tight, little Bernie is sleepy . . . . [Sits up.] Little Bernie is not sleepy!

[Pause, then he yells very loudly]

GRANNY!!!!!! GRANNY!!!!! GRANNY!!!!!!

GRANNY: [Enters, all out of breath.] What is it now, Bernie? Your poor old Granny is getting plum tuckered out.

BERNIE BEAR: I tried to sing myself some lullabies. The boys and girls sang me some lullabies, but you know what I really, really, really need?

GRANNY: What do you really, really, really need, Bernie Bear?

BERNIE BEAR: Well, what I really, really, really need is for YOU to sing me a lullaby. Then, I think I can go to sleep.

GRANNY: Alright. I'll sing you a lullaby. Granny loves to sing her little Bernie Bear a nighty-night song and send him off to dreamland.

BERNIE BEAR: Oh boy! Granny is gonna sing me a lullaby so I can go to sleep! Sing me "Rock a Bye Bernie" please, Granny.

GRANNY: That's a very fine idea. Then I'll be able to go downstairs and catch the end of my favorite movie. Because I'm getting very tired from running up and down these stairs.

> Rock-a-bye Bernie,
>
> On the tree top.
>
> When the wind blows, . . . [She starts singing slower.]
>
> The cradle will rock . . . .
>
> When the . . . bough . . . breaks, [She sings more slowly.]
>
> The cradle will fall . . . ,
>
> And down will come . . . Bernie . . . [She falls asleep and
> starts to snore.]

[Snore, snore. . .]

[Mutters.] Cradle . . .

[Snore, snore, . . .]

[Pause.]

BERNIE BEAR: [Whispering.] Granny . . . Granny . . .[Pokes her.] Are you sleeping?

GRANNY: [Snore, Snore, . . .]

BERNIE BEAR: Oh, I think Granny fell asleep. I better go downstairs and sleep on the sofa and let Granny have my bed and my cuddly and my blankie. Night-night, Granny. [Gives Granny a kiss and exits.]

GRANNY: [Snore, snore.]

The End

LITERACY TO GO

Dear Parents and Caregivers,

We enjoyed having you and your children attend our storytime today. We tried to get Bernie Bear sleepy by singing him some lullabies in our puppet show, "Bedtime for Bernie Bear." Today's Literacy To Go tip is about singing with your child. Singing breaks words into syllables. This helps children begin to differentiate the sounds that make up our language. This skill, called *phonological awareness*, supports early literacy development.

Here are the words to the songs we sang at storytime today, so you can sing them with your child at home. Don't worry about perfect pitch; kids love to sing and to be sung to.

Twinkle, Twinkle, Little Star

Twinkle, twinkle, little star,

How I wonder what you are.

Up above the world so high,

Like a diamond in the sky.

Twinkle, twinkle, little star,

How I wonder what you are.

Little Bo-Peep

Little Bo-Peep has lost her sheep,

And doesn't know where to find them.

Leave them alone and they will come home,

Wagging their tails behind them.

Baa, Baa, Black Sheep Have You Any Wool?

Baa, baa, black sheep, have you any wool?

Yes, sir, yes, sir, three bags full.

One for my master, one for my dame,

And one for the little boy who lives down the lane.

See you next week!

Literacy To Go Take Home Menu

Books that build phonological awareness and involve singing: These books contain the words to popular songs. You can sing them as you read them. You'll also enjoy the colorful illustrations. Have fun!

Bates, Ivan. *Five Little Ducks.*

Cabrera, Jane. *Ten in the Bed.*

Canyon, Christopher. *John Denver's "Take Me Home, Country Roads".*

Montgomery, Wayne. *Over the Candlestick: Classic Nursery Rhymes and the Real Stories Behind Them.*

Nursery Songs and Lullabies.
    Featuring the art of Bessie Pease Gutmann.

Pinkney, J Brian. *Hush Little Baby.*

Trapani, Iza. *Baa Baa Black Sheep, Froggie Went A-Courtin', Here We Go 'Round the Mulberry Bush, I'm a Little Teapot, The Itsy Bitsy Spider, Oh Where, Oh Where Has My Little Dog Gone?, Row, Row, Row Your Boat, Shoo Fly!, and Twinkle, Twinkle Little Star.*

Warhola, James. *If You're Happy and You Know It.*

Yarrow, Pete and Leonard Lipton. *Puff, the Magic Dragon.*

Traditional Songs [series]. Edited by Ann Owen. Minneapolis, MN: Picture Window Books, 2003– . Titles include:

The Ants Go Marching	*I Know an Old Lady*
Clementine	*I've Been Working on the Railroad*
The Farmer in the Dell	*She'll Be Coming Around the Mountain*

From *Puppet Plays Plus: Using Stock Characters to Entertain and Teach Early Literacy* by Laurel L. Iakovakis. Westport, CT: Libraries Unlimited. Copyright © 2009.

You're Invited to a
PUPPET SHOW!
Come to storytime and a special
puppet show performance of

BEDTIME FOR
BERNIE BEAR

Bernie Bear can't wait to have Granny come to babysit. But, oh no! It's bedtime and Bernie, no matter how hard he tries, just cannot get to sleep. We'll sing him some lullabies and songs for quiet time. Will that help Bernie fall asleep? Join us to find out.

To share in the fun, **bring your own stuffed animal** to storytime this week.

Our puppet show is specially designed for children ages three through eight and their parents. It will help build phonological awareness through music.

Date (and day of week): _____

At (library name & address, room number or area)

_____

Bring your favorite stuffed animal with you!

BERNIE BEAR'S BIRTHDAY

Related Themes: Birthdays, Grandparents, Presents, Rhyming

Overview: The letter "B" plays a prominent role in this storytime, as indicated in the show's title. Decorate the room with a birthday theme. Before the puppet show, you may talk about the letter "B," and words and names that begin with that letter.

Words that sound alike and have a similar rhythm pattern provide the humor in the puppet show. It's Bernie's birthday, and Granny wants to give him the perfect gift. But poor Granny keeps misunderstanding the gifts that Bernie requests.

Early Literacy Skill Focus: *Letter knowledge* is a component of this show. The letter "B" is a feature of the show, as indicated by the alliteration in the title. Granny talks about "B" when she thinks Bernie wants a spelling lesson.

When Granny misunderstands the presents Bernie Bear wants for his birthday, she hears another word that sounds similar. This gives you the opportunity to discuss *phonological awareness*, specifically words that rhyme or have a similar rhythm pattern.

Other Literacy Opportunities:

- **Phonological awareness:** The puppet show features words and phrases that sound alike and have a similar rhythm pattern. For example, Bernie asks Granny for a "parakeet," and she thinks he says a "pair of keys." The audience will be asked to help Bernie tell Granny what he wants for his birthday presents. They will use the words from the script that sound alike, such as "ice cream cone" and "big dog bone." This is a rhyming skill associated with *phonological awareness.*

    If you plan to talk about these words before the puppet show, you may wish to print some pictures from the Internet. You can show the audience the pictures, clap syllables together, and/or say the words aloud together to hear the similarities.

- **Letter knowledge:** Letter knowledge, specifically the letter "B," is the primary focus of the puppet show. The title of the puppet show is "Bernie Bear's Birthday," and all words start with the letter "B." Prepare the storytime space to reflect the birthday theme and to give a festive feel to your storytime. Decorate the puppet stage with a "Happy Birthday" banner.

    The Literacy To Go sheet offers titles that feature the letter "B" and other titles that offer letter knowledge skill development opportunities.

Materials Needed:

- Puppets: Bernie Bear, Granny.

- Props: Two keys on a chain, carrot, old dish, big dog bone, birthday cake (made from an oatmeal box; see p. 63).

- Early literacy activity:

    – "Happy Birthday" banner (purchased from a party store).

    – Foam, magnetic, or die-cut letter "B" (can be found at a craft store).

    – Optional: You may wish to print color pictures off the Internet of the gifts that Bernie asks for and the ones he receives instead. In other words, print a picture of a parrot and a carrot—or use the carrot prop from the show. You may hold the pictures side by side before or after the show to allow the audience to repeat the similar sounding words.

- Literacy To Go handouts for participants (see pp. 60–61).

- Promotional flyers (see p. 62).

- Display books for checkout; use titles provided on the Literacy To Go handout.

- Titles for read-alouds.

- Birthday cards and die cuts of the letter "B" (like confetti) to decorate the display table.

Preparation:

A few weeks or more before the program

– Decide on your storytime program theme.

– Announce storytime program in the library Web site and newsletter.

– Reproduce the promotional flyer (p. 62) and distribute copies to caregivers at the library.

– Make the birthday cake prop (see p. 63).

A week or two before the program

- Select and gather your read-aloud titles, as well as display books for checkout, puppets, and props.
- Make or purchase foam, magnetic, or die-cut letter "B" to show to the audience.
- Gather Literacy To Go display items, such as die cuts of the letter "B" and colorful birthday cards.
- Reproduce the Literacy To Go materials (see pp. 60–61).
- Practice the read-alouds and the puppet play.

On the day of the program

- Create a display of checkout material based on the phonological awareness theme of rhyming verse.
- Decorate the Literacy To Go display table with the birthday cards and die cut letter "B."
- Decorate the puppet stage with the "Happy Birthday" banner

Puppet Show Performance Tips: After finishing with each prop, bring it backstage. You don't want to have too many props on the stage.

It may be necessary to prompt the audience more than once to repeat after Bernie Bear. You may have him tell the audience, "Granny still didn't hear that. Let's say it again, only louder."

The Program

During the read-aloud segment: Use the Bernie Bear puppet to welcome the participants and to gather the children and caregivers into a semicircle around your storytelling chair. Have the Bernie Bear puppet tell the audience that it's his birthday and that his name starts with the letter "B."

You may use the letter "B" in the word birthday to begin talking about the letter B. For example, you may say, "Birthday begins with the letter 'B,' just like Bernie Bear. Does anyone here have a name that starts with 'B'?" Tell parents that occasionally pointing out letters as they read will help children develop knowledge of the alphabet. Tell them that using alphabet books that have clear block letters will reinforce this skill. Alphabet books that use flashy and showy print will also help with the skill of print awareness, as the print is more prominent on the page and offers opportunities to follow along with your finger as you read.

After reading your selected literature, talk about some of the rhyming words from the puppet show. If you printed Internet pictures of the birthday gift requests, show a few of them now. Show the big dog bone prop and a picture of an ice cream cone. Say the words, emphasizing the rhyme and the rhythm pattern. This helps prepare the children for the puppet show. Inform parents that playing rhyming games like this helps children understand sounds, which is a prereading skill called phonological awareness.

Introduce the puppet show: Stand in front of the puppet stage with the Bernie Bear puppet on your hand. Use Bernie Bear to excitedly announce the title of the puppet show. He may show the audience a die cut, foam, or magnetic letter "B." Point to the letter "B" on the birthday banner. Have Bernie gather the group around the puppet stage.

After the group is assembled comfortably around the puppet stage, as leader, address the group with the following welcome.

You can see that Bernie Bear is very excited to be having a birthday. Granny is coming over to celebrate with him. He asks Granny for some presents that he would like to have for his birthday, but Granny, who doesn't hear very well, keeps misunderstanding him. She brings him some silly presents. We'll have to wait until the end to see if Bernie gets anything that he wants.

I better stop talking! Bernie is getting anxious to see what he gets for his birthday presents. So am I! Let's find out.

Move to your place behind the puppet stage to begin the show.

After the puppet show: With the children, sing a happy birthday song to Bernie Bear.

Talk about other words that start with the letter "B", such as names of the children in the room, blue things in the room, books, boys, buckle, etc.

Encourage caregivers to check out the display titles and to pick up a copy of the Literacy To Go sheet.

Have the puppets tell the children good-bye.

BERNIE BEAR'S BIRTHDAY

Puppets:

Bernie Bear

Granny

Props:

Two keys on a chain

Carrot

Old dish

Big dog bone (white dog bone purchased from pet store)

Birthday cake (made from an oatmeal box; see instructions on p. 63)

[Enter Bernie Bear.]

BERNIE BEAR: OOOOHHHHH BOY!!! It's my birthday! [In a sing-songy voice.] I'm so excited! I can hardly wait! Happy Birthday to me. Happy Birthday to me. OOOOHHHH!!! I'm so excited! My granny is coming to see me for my birthday. I have a whole list of presents I'm going to ask for! OOOOHHHH! [To audience.] Do you think my granny will get me a nice present for my birthday? I sure hope so!

GRANNY: Yoo-hoo!

BERNIE BEAR: That must be Granny!

GRANNY: [Offstage.] Bernie! Oh, Bernie Bear! Where's my Bernie Bear Birthday Boy? Bernie!

BERNIE BEAR: [Calls to her.] Granny! I'm upstairs. Come up and see me.

GRANNY: [Enters the stage with her back to the audience.] Bernie? Bernie? Where are you? I can't see you.

BERNIE BEAR: Granny, turn around. I'm right here.

GRANNY: Oh, there you are Bernie Bear! How's my birthday boy? Come and give your granny a hug and a kiss.

[They hug and kiss, make kissing sounds.]

I can't believe that my little Bernie Bear is having another birthday. Have you been thinking about what gift you want your granny to get for you?

BERNIE BEAR: Oh boy! [In a sing-songy voice.] I'm so excited. My granny's gonna buy me a birthday present. Thank you, Granny. I have a whole long list of things I want! My granny's gonna buy me a birthday present!

GRANNY: What's that, Bernie? I didn't hear what you said.

BERNIE BEAR: I said, "Thank you. I want a birthday present!"

GRANNY: EH? You said you want a spelling lesson? Well, back in my day, I was quite the spelling bee champion. All-righty, if you want to have a spelling lesson, then that's what I'll give you. Let's start with words that start with "B," just like Bernie Bear's Birthday.

BERNIE BEAR: NO! Not a spelling lesson, a birthday present! [To audience.] My poor granny doesn't hear very well.

GRANNY: There's the words ball, book, big, . . . they all start with the letter "B."

BERNIE BEAR: GRANNY! . . . I would like A PRESENT FOR MY BIRTHDAY!

GRANNY: Blue, box . . . .

BERNIE BEAR: Boys and girls, can you help me? Let's all tell Granny, that I want a birthday present! Can you help me? I'll count to three and then we'll all say, "Bernie wants a birthday present!" Okay . . . one, two, three . . . .

[Bernie and audience say:] "Bernie wants a birthday present!"

GRANNY: And there's the word bug and boy. . . . EH? What's that? You want a birthday present? Not a spelling lesson? There's not any need to shout! I can hear you just fine! Why sure I'll buy you a birthday present, Bernie Bear. What would you like?

BERNIE BEAR: Oh thank you, Granny! Thank you, boys and girls. OOOOHHHH boy! I'm so excited. Granny's gonna get me a birthday present!

Well, Granny, you know how much I love animals. So I was hoping maybe you would get me a little bird. Maybe I could have a parakeet. My mommy said it was okay. I really want a parakeet. Please, please, Granny, may I have a parakeet?

GRANNY: That seems like a silly present, but I can get you two of those.

BERNIE BEAR: Wow! Two of them?

GRANNY: Of course two, because a pair means two—you know, a pair of shoes, a pair of socks, that means two shoes, two socks. What you want with a pair of keys, I'll never know. But wait right here, I'll get them now. [She exits.]

BERNIE BEAR: [To audience.] Oh, my goodness! I asked Granny for a parakeet and she thought I said a pair of keys! Sometimes Granny doesn't hear very well. Oh, I don't really want a pair of keys.

GRANNY: [Reenters with two keys on a key chain.] Here they are. Just as you wanted. A pair of keys. See, one key, two keys . . . a pair of keys. Happy birthday, Bernie! Come and give your granny a hug!

[They hug.]

BERNIE BEAR: Granny, I didn't say a pair of keys, I said a parakeet. You know, so I can listen to the little bird sing and watch it fly around in its cage. Oh, dear. My poor Granny doesn't hear very well.

Boys and girls, can you help me tell Granny that I want a parakeet, not a pair of keys? When I count to three, let's all say, "Bernie wants a parakeet, not a pair of keys!"

Ready? One, two, three . . .

[Bernie and audience say:] "Bernie wants a parakeet, not a pair of keys!"

GRANNY: EH? You say a parakeet, not a pair of keys? Well, I wondered why you would want a pair of keys. That was kind of a silly present. Okay, we'll put a parakeet on our shopping list. Is there anything else that Granny can get you for a birthday present?

BERNIE BEAR: Well, after you mentioned two birds, I would really like to also have a parrot. Granny, could you get me a parrot? My mommy loves parrots, too. I can teach it to talk. Granny, can you get me a parrot?

GRANNY: My clever little Bernie Bear. Always eats his vegetables. Of course I'll get you a carrot. A carrot isn't much of a birthday present, but if that is what my Bernie Bear wants, that is what he's going to get. Especially a carrot. Carrots are good for you. Wait right here. [She exits.]

BERNIE BEAR: [Calls to Granny.] I said parrot, not carrot! Oh, dear! Granny doesn't hear very well. [To audience.] When my granny comes back, we're going to have to tell her that I said parrot, not carrot. I do like carrots, but not for a birthday present!

GRANNY: [Reenters with a carrot.] Here's your carrot! Happy Birthday, Bernie!

BERNIE BEAR: Thank you, Granny. But I said parrot, not carrot. You know, one of those big colorful birds that talk.

GRANNY: I never heard of a colorful carrot, just orange.

BERNIE BEAR: Boys and girls, let's try again. When I count to three, let's all tell Granny, "Bernie wants a parrot, not a carrot!" Okay? One, two, three . . . .

[Bernie and audience say:] "Bernie wants a parrot, not a carrot!"

GRANNY: EH? You said parrot? Not carrot? Well, that makes more sense. I thought you were getting a little rattle-brained. Let's put a parrot on our shopping list.

BERNIE BEAR: Okay. And I'll eat that carrot with my lunch, okay, Granny?

GRANNY: You bet. But first, what can Granny get you for your birthday present?

BERNIE BEAR: Maybe I should try one more animal. What do you think, boys and girls? I'll ask Granny for a goldfish. Maybe this time you should all help me ask Granny. Let's all say, "Bernie wants a goldfish." Ready . . . one, two, three . . . .

[Bernie and audience say:] "Bernie wants a goldfish!"

GRANNY: You don't have to holler! That's easy! I don't even have to buy one because I've got his favorite one right down in the kitchen. [She exits.]

BERNIE BEAR: [To audience.] Uh-oh! Granny doesn't have a goldfish in the kitchen. I wonder what she's talking about. I wonder what she's going to bring me next.

GRANNY: [Reenters with an old dish.] Here you go! Here's your old dish. Your favorite old dish. I remember when you ate your first bite of solid food from this dish. It was adorable. And now you're such a big boy! And having another birthday! But an old dish is not much of a birthday present . . . .

Oh, wait a second! I know why you wanted an old dish for your birthday. To use it to eat your carrot. But Bernie, you should ask me for a better present than that silly thing.

BERNIE BEAR: I said goldfish, not old dish. [To audience.] My poor Granny doesn't hear very well. We'll try again, I'll count to three and we'll all say, "Bernie wants a goldfish, not an old dish!" One, two, three . . . .

[Bernie and audience say:] "Bernie wants a goldfish, not an old dish!"

GRANNY: Oh for heaven's sake! Of course you said a goldfish, not an old dish! My goodness, you're going to have a house full of critters, but let's put that on our shopping list. Okay, Bernie, what else, this is fun!

BERNIE BEAR: Another present?

GRANNY: Yes, another present.

BERNIE BEAR: Well, maybe I should just ask for something very simple, like maybe, we could go out and have an ice cream cone.

GRANNY: EH? What was that?

BERNIE BEAR: I said, "An ice cream cone."

GRANNY: I think you are tricking your Granny. I'll be right back. [She exits.]

BERNIE BEAR: [To audience.] Hmmm . . . I wonder what she thought I said this time. Because you know, my poor granny doesn't hear very well. What do you think? A telephone? That rhymes with ice cream cone. Calzone? Small stone? Trip to Rome? You never know with my granny!

GRANNY: [Enters with big dog bone.] Here you are, Bernie Bear! A big dog bone, just like you asked for. Now I guess you want a puppy dog, too?

BERNIE BEAR: Of course I want a puppy. But my mommy said I have to wait until I'm older. But I didn't say "big dog bone," I said, "ice cream cone."

GRANNY: What's that? A cell phone?

BERNIE BEAR: No! Boys and girls, help me again! Let's all tell Granny, "Bernie wants an ice cream cone, not a big dog bone!" Okay, one, two, three . . . .

[Bernie and audience say:] "Bernie wants an ice cream cone, not a big dog bone!"

GRANNY: Oh! An ice cream cone. I will get you an ice cream cone when we go to the pet store. That'll be a fun afternoon. We'll get an ice cream cone, then we'll go find a parakeet and a parrot and a goldfish.

Now, Granny is getting tired of going up and down all these stairs. Why don't you pick out one more present, and Granny will get it for you for your birthday.

BERNIE BEAR: [To audience.] Let's see, first I wanted a parakeet and Granny got me a pair of keys. Then I asked for a parrot and she gave me a carrot. Then, I tried a goldfish and she gave me an old dish. Then I asked for an ice cream cone and Granny got me a big dog bone. I think she's been playing some tricks on me, so maybe we can play a trick on Granny. I'm going to ask her to get me a big green snake. That's what I'm going to do. Will you help me ask Granny for a big green snake?

When I count to three, let's all say, "Bernie wants a big green snake." Can we say that? This is going to be funny! Granny is afraid of snakes. "Bernie wants a big green snake." Ready? One, two, three . . . .

[Bernie and audience say:] "Bernie wants a big green snake!"

Ha, ha, ha. Let's see what she does now! What do you say, Granny? Will you get me a big green snake?

GRANNY: Thank goodness! Finally, Bernie, you ask me for something sensible.

BERNIE BEAR: You think that a big green snake is a good present?

GRANNY: Of course I do. I think it's the best present of all. [She exits.]

BERNIE BEAR: [To audience.] What now???? I don't think she'll really get me a big green snake, do you?

GRANNY: [Reenters with birthday cake.] Happy birthday, Bernie Bear! Granny makes the best birthday cake!

BERNIE BEAR: Silly me! I should have known! When I said big green snake, Granny thought that I said birthday cake! Granny, you are right. This is the best present of all. I didn't really want a big green snake, but I really did want a birthday cake! Thank you, thank you, thank you!

GRANNY: Yep, your old Granny knows what's best! Let's go downstairs and eat a piece, what do you say, Bernie Bear?

BERNIE BEAR: I say yummy in my tummy! Let's go.

The End

LITERACY TO GO

Dear Parents and Caregivers,

We enjoyed having you and your children attend our storytime today. Listening to books, attending library activities, and participating in the joy of literature is a necessary step to creating a generation of literate students and adults. It is never too early to make yourself an active educational partner for the future of your child.

The title of today's puppet show was "Bernie Bear's Birthday." All of these words start with the letter "B." You can help your child become aware of letters by talking about the alphabet. This is a skill known as letter knowledge. Next time you are in the grocery store, talk about all the food items you see that start with the letter B. You'll be amazed how many you can spot!

Today's puppet show also featured multisyllabic words that sound alike and have similar rhythm. Practicing sounds is a prereading skill known as phonological awareness. Play rhyming games with your child. Start by rhyming some of the words we used today. What other words rhyme with "cone," "snake," and "parrot?" Nonsense words are okay, too!

The list below also contains titles and text that feature the letter B. Also included are alphabet books that you will enjoy. As you read some of these books together, occasionally point to the letter B when it appears in print.

See you next week!

 ## Literacy To Go Take Home Menu

Books that build letter knowledge and focus on the letter "B": The letter B is featured frequently in the text and/or titles of these engaging read-alouds.

Anderson, Derek. *Gladys Goes Out to Lunch.*
    Gladys is a gorilla who spices up her diet
    by discovering banana bread.

Bruss, Deborah. *Book! Book! Book!*
    Farm animals discover the joy of reading.

McPhail, David. *Big Brown Bear's Birthday Surprise.*
    A big brown bear's friend, Rat, is giving
    him a birthday present that has four letters
    and starts with a "B."

Mitton, Tony. *Busy Boats.*
    All kinds of boats and what they are used
    for.

Patricelli, Leslie. *The Birthday Box.*
    An imaginative child finds many uses for a box.

Books for more letter knowledge: The ABCs are effectively introduced in the following alphabet books.

Blackstone, Stella. *Cleo's Alphabet Book.*
    Clues are given for readers to guess the
    object described.

Cleary, Brian P. *Peanut Butter and Jellyfishes:
A Very Silly Alphabet Book.*
    Search the pages to find the alphabet letters,
    words that start with the letters, and silly rhymes.

Delessert, Etienne. *Aa: A Was an Apple Pie, an English Nursery Rhyme.*
> Clear text, upper and lower case letters, and imaginative pictures make this book a winner.

Dog Artlist Collection (Firm). *The Dog from Arf! Arf! to Zzzzzz.*
> The reader may not intuitively know the letter of the alphabet being represented, but dog lovers will want to examine this book.

Lobel, Anita. *Animal Antics: A to Z.*
> Animals, animal sounds, and letters in one fun book.

MacDonald, Ross. *Achoo! Bang! Crash!: A Noisy Alphabet.*
> An interactive alphabet book; make sounds while learning letters.

Marino, Gianna. *Zoopa: An Alphabet Soup ABC.*
> A simple bowl of tomato soup evolves as each page introduces another animal and the antics to go along with it.

Meddaugh, Susan. *Martha Speaks.*
> Not an alphabet book, but this talking dog offers an excellent way to bring attention to letters of the alphabet.

O'Keefe, Susan Heyboer. *Hungry Monster ABC.*
> Wonderful and funny illustrations with loveable monsters.

Pallotta, Jerry. *The Construction Alphabet Book.*
> Construction vehicles from the well known to the little known.

Pearson, Debora. *Alphabeep: A Zipping, Zooming ABC.*
> Vehicles from ambulance to zamboni, with the sounds to go along with them.

Wallace, Nancy Elizabeth. *Alphabet House.*
> Connects objects found in everyday life, with their first letter. Colors also.

You're Invited to a
PUPPET SHOW!
Come to storytime and a special puppet show performance of

BERNIE BEAR'S BIRTHDAY

Bernie Bear is excited to see what present Granny will get him for his birthday. But poor Granny keeps misunderstanding Bernie and tries to give him the wrong gifts. Will Bernie get the present he really wants?

Our puppet show is specially designed for children three to eight and their parents. We'll have fun helping Granny understand what Bernie is trying to tell her. Playing around with the sounds of words helps build phonological awareness, an important early literacy skill. We will play with rhymes and rhythms in this funny puppet show.

Date (and day of week): _____

At (library name & address, room number or area)

_____

Come to Bernie's Birthday!

Making a Birthday Cake from an Oatmeal Box

Materials needed:

Empty 18 oz. oatmeal cylinder

White felt

Colorful yarn

Acrylic paint

Birthday candles

One 7-inch paper plate

Hot glue and glue gun

Cut the oatmeal cylinder into a 3-inch-tall cylinder. Wrap it in white felt and hot glue it into place. Use colorful yarn and acrylic paint to decorate the cake. Hot glue candles onto the top of cylinder. Hot glue the decorated cylinder onto 7-inch paper plate.

MOOSTERPIECE THEATER: CLEVER PIGGY RAE AND THE BIG BAD WOLF

Related Themes: Halloween, Fairy tales, Wolves, Pigs

Overview: This puppet show focuses on building phonological, or sound, awareness by using repetitive text. Throughout the show, children are asked to repeat two popular lines from "The Three Little Pigs."

In the puppet show, the Big Bad Wolf tries to trick Piggy Rae into "letting him come in" by wearing various Halloween costumes. The characters sing and introduce new vocabulary words. The children in the audience are called upon to advise Piggy Rae whether she should open the door for the costumed Big Bad Wolf.

Early Literacy Skill Focus: The main literacy skill focused on, and the skill reinforced on the Literacy To Go sheet at the end of this chapter, is *phonological awareness*, specifically through repetitive text. The booklist on the Literacy To Go sheet comprises books that repeat a phrase throughout.

In addition, by writing and referring to the words in the "Big Bad Wolf" song, you bring attention to the printed word, helping children to develop *print awareness*.

Other Literacy Opportunities:

- **Vocabulary:** Vocabulary words introduced in this puppet show include *clever*, *outsmart*, *traditional*, *outwit*, and *paranoid*.

- **Phonological awareness:** This script and Literacy To Go take home tips support phonological awareness through the use of repetitive text. During the introduction and throughout the show, the audience repeats two popular phrases from "The Three Little Pigs": "Little pig, little pig let me come in" and "Not by the hair on my chinny-chin-chin."

  The puppets also sing songs based on popular tunes. The final song, the "Big Bad Wolf" song, can be sung by everyone after the puppet show. Singing is another method to help build the early literacy skill of phonological awareness.

- **Print awareness:** Before the puppet show, point out to the audience that you have written two lines from "The Three Little Pigs" and the words to the "Big Bad Wolf" song on an easel/wipe-off board. Tell the audience that the words are there because they will be repeating them during the puppet show.

  Also tell them that you will be singing the "Big Bad Wolf" song. Inform the children that the words are displayed so their parents can read along while you sing the song. Point out the letter "B" in "Big" and "Bad" (words used throughout the song) to add the element of *letter knowledge*.

- **Narrative skills:** Most adults know the story of "The Three Little Pigs." Encourage parents to read a version of this story to their child at home, summarize it, and then have their children tell it back to them. Telling and retelling stories develops the narrative skill and opens opportunities for vocabulary development.

Materials Needed:

- Puppets: Alistair McMoose, Piggy Rae (wearing her pink feather boa), Wolf.

- Props for the show: Hardback book and ruler or spoon (to make a knocking sound, unseen by audience), eye patch and blond wig for wolf puppet. (Purchase or make yourself; instructions on p. 81.)

- Halloween display pieces (black cats, jack-o-lanterns, etc.) to decorate the Literacy To Go table.

- Easel or wipe-off board:

  – Write the words "Little pig, little pig, let me come in."
  – Write the words "Not by the hair on my chinny-chin-chin."
  – Write the words to the "Big Bad Wolf" song (see script, p. 77).

- Display books for checkout; use titles provided on the Literacy To Go handout.

- Literacy To Go handouts for participants (see pp. 78–79).

- Promotional flyers (see p. 80).

- Titles for read-alouds.

Preparation:

A few weeks or more before the program

  – Decide on your program theme.

- Announce the storytime program in the library Web site and newsletter.
- Reproduce the promotional flyer (p. 80) and distribute copies to caregivers at the library.
- If making the props yourself, follow directions on p. 81.

A week or two before the program

- Select and gather your read-aloud titles, display books for checkout, puppets, and props.
- Write the words to the song and repetitive phrases from the puppet show on the easel or wipe-off board.
- Reproduce the Literacy To Go materials (see pp. 78–79).
- Practice the read-aloud books and the puppet play.

On the day of the program

- Create a display of checkout material based on the phonological awareness theme of repetitive text.
- Decorate the table with Halloween paraphernalia.
- Put up the easel or wipe-off board with text from script and words to the song written on it.

Puppet Show Performance Tips: It takes a bit of practice to get the puppets up and down quickly when it is their turn to be on stage. Be sure to rehearse these scenes to make them flow well.

Listen for laughter from the audience, and don't speak over it. The scene in which the wolf has on the wig usually gets a hearty laugh.

Take a hardback book behind the puppet stage with you. You'll need it to make the knocking sound when the Big Bad Wolf knocks on Piggy Rae's door. Use a ruler or spoon to knock on the book, because you will have puppets on your hands.

If the audience forgets to repeat their line, have the puppet remind them. If only a few people in the audience remember, give them another chance by having the puppet say, "Come on, you can do better than that!" Then feed the line to them again.

The Program

During the read-aloud segment: After welcoming the participants, gather the children and caregivers into a semicircle around your storytelling chair. Between read-alouds, talk about the vocabulary words, the song written on the easel or wipe-off board, or any of the other literacy skills listed above.

Introduce the puppet show: Have the group assemble comfortably around the puppet stage. As leader, address the group with the following welcome.

> Do you all remember the story of "The Three Little Pigs?" Have you ever wondered what happened after the Big Bad Wolf could not blow down the third little pig's brick house? Did he give up? Or did he come back to try again? Maybe he waited until Halloween, then put on a disguise and tried to trick the third little pig into "letting him come in!"
>
> Today's show is called "Clever Piggy Rae and the Big Bad Wolf." What does the word "clever" mean? (Wait for audience to respond.) That's right. "Clever" means smart. We already know that Piggy Rae is gorgeous and talented. Do you think she is clever, or smart, also? (Wait for audience to respond.)

You could be right. Piggy Rae will need your help to be smart. Listen for the Big Bad Wolf to say, "Little pig, little pig, let me come in!" When he does, we want you to repeat those words again. Let's practice. I'll say, "Little pig, little pig, let me come in!" Now you repeat it. (Wait.) Great!

Who remembers what the pig says next? She says, "Not by the hair on my chinny-chin-chin!" You are going to say that right after Piggy Rae says it. Let's practice. I'll say, "Not by the hair on my chinny-chin-chin!" Now you repeat it. (Wait.) Great!

You're very good! Thank you. The puppets will give you another opportunity to practice.

Have fun with our show.

Move to your place behind the puppet stage to begin the show.

After the puppet show: Sing the "Big Bad Wolf" song with the whole group. Stand in front of the puppet stage with the puppets on your hands, and have the puppets sing along as you did in the script.

Explain to caregivers that reading books that have a repeating phrase helps to develop the early literacy skill of phonological awareness. Tell them that you have chosen titles for the display that have repetitive text.

Encourage caregivers to check out the display titles and to pick up a copy of the Literacy To Go sheet.

Parents may retell this story at home and have their children retell it to them.

Have the puppets tell the children good-bye.

MOOSTERPIECE THEATER: CLEVER PIGGY RAE AND THE BIG BAD WOLF

Puppets:

> Alistair McMoose
>
> Piggy Rae (wearing her pink feather boa)
>
> Wolf

Props:

> Hardback book and ruler or spoon (not seen by audience): Used to make a knocking sound by rapping on the book with the ruler or spoon.
>
> Eye patch for Big Bad Wolf (purchase, or see p. 81 for instructions on how to make this prop yourself).
>
> Blond wig for Big Bad Wolf (purchase, or see p. 81 for instructions on how to make this prop yourself).

[Enter Alistair McMoose.]

ALISTAIR McMOOSE: Good morning, boys and girls. Welcome to *Moosterpiece Theater*—way, way, way off Broadway theater. I am your host, Alistair McMoose. Let me begin by wishing all of you a Happy Halloween, as we begin today's performance of "Clever Piggy Rae and the Big Bad Wolf." We will feature Piggy Rae starring as the Clever Little Pig and the Big Bad Wolf starring as himself. Do you know what the word "clever" means? [Pause for audience to respond.] That's right, "clever" means smart. With your help, Piggy Rae will use her wits to outsmart the Big Bad Wolf.

[Enter Piggy Rae.]

PIGGY RAE: Hi! Happy Halloween, y'all!! It is I, Piggy Rae. Famous way, way, way off Broadway actress. Y'all are so lucky that you will get to see me perform today.

ALISTAIR McMOOSE: Piggy Rae, I am perfectly capable of introducing the cast without your help. Please wait until the show begins.

PIGGY RAE: I know Alistair, but I knew that my fans could hardly wait to see me. Don't go away, y'all. I'll be right back. [She exits.]

ALISTAIR McMOOSE: Oh, dear. As you can imagine, this will be way, way, way bad theater, very bad indeed. This is just a sign of things to come . . . .

We need your help today.

I'm sure all of you know the traditional story of "The Three Little Pigs." They each built a house—and one by one the Big Bad Wolf knocked on their doors, trying to get inside. He blew down the house made of hay and the house made of sticks, but was unable to blow down the house made of bricks. Our story takes place on Halloween night, and the Big Bad Wolf is still trying to trick the third little pig.

[Enter Piggy Rae.]

PIGGY RAE: Alistair! How you do go on! You are boring these children to death! Blah, blah, blah, . . . Let me help you out. Boys and girls, when the Big Bad Wolf comes to my house and knocks on my door he says, "Little pig, little pig, let me come in!" I need y'all to repeat that line every time you hear it, so I can really hear it! And then when I say, "Not by the hair on my chinny-chin-chin," you repeat after me, so the wolf can hear what I'm saying. I'm counting on you. [She exits.]

ALISTAIR McMOOSE: Well, she certainly knows how to cut to the chase, doesn't she? Before we begin, let's do a small practice. Let's hear a round of applause for the Big Bad Wolf. Yeaaah!

[Enter Big Bad Wolf, exit Alistair.]

BIG BAD WOLF: [Use a voice that makes you sound as if your nose is stuffed up.] Yes, yes, I know, it is difficult to applaud for the Big Bad Wolf, but, the show must go on. Boys and girls, whenever you hear me say, "Little pig, little pig, let me come in!" you are to repeat it, using your best Big Bad Wolf voice. Let's practice. [Make knocking sound.]

"Little pig, little pig, let me come in!"

[Audience repeats:] "Little pig, little pig, let me come in!"

Oh, my! Very good, very scary, very wolfy. Bravo! Once more for the road!

[Make knocking sound.]

"Little pig, little pig, let me come in!"

[Audience repeats:] "Little pig, little pig, let me come in!"

You are all very talented. See you later!

[Enter Alistair, exit Big Bad Wolf.]

ALISTAIR McMOOSE: I'm shivering inside. That was bone-chilling. Now of course, Piggy Rae will need her turn to practice with you. Let's bring her on, the talented, adorable, and very pink, Piggy Rae. Yeaaah!

[Enter Piggy Rae, exit Alistair.]

PIGGY RAE: Thank you, Alistair, thank you, fans! So when you repeat my line after me, you will be using your most adorable Piggy Rae voice possible. But let me clear something up before we go on. I DO NOT have any hair on my chinny-chin-chin. We're talking Piggy Rae here, so let's just get that straight. Pink, adorable, talented, gorgeous, and NO HAIRY CHIN, Piggy Rae. Famous way, way, way off Broadway actress . . . .

[Enter Alistair.]

ALISTAIR McMOOSE: Piggy Rae! Let's get on with it! [He exits.]

PIGGY RAE: Very well, but don't go looking for any hair on my adorable chin. Okay boys and girls, when I say, "Not by the hair on my chinny-chin-chin!" you repeat it after me. Let's practice. "Not by the hair on my chinny-chin-chin."

[Audience repeats:] "Not by the hair on my chinny-chin-chin."

PIGGY RAE: Y'all are very good! Not as talented as I, Piggy Rae, of course, but with some proper coaching, you may have a future as off, off, off Broadway stars.

So, boys and girls, are you ready to begin?

[Allow time for audience to respond.]

PIGGY RAE: Great, so am I. [Calls out.] Alistair! Let's get this show on the road!

[Exit Piggy Rae, enter Alistair.]

ALISTAIR McMOOSE: And now, without further ado, we will begin our *Moosterpiece Theater* performance of "Clever Piggy Rae and the Big Bad Wolf."

[Enter Piggy Rae, exit Alistair.]

PIGGY RAE: [Singing to the tune of Handel's "Hallelujah Chorus."] Bellybutton, bellybutton, bellybutton, belly-but-ton! Hi y'all! As you know, I am famous for many things, including singing the Bellybutton Opera which was my talent in the Miss Pork Rind Beauty Contest in 2001.

Since it is Halloween, I am getting ready for all the trick-or-treaters to come to my house tonight, all dressed up in their adorable little costumes. BUT . . . I know that the Big Bad Wolf lives down the street! If he comes here, I will not let him in.

Oh, y'all, I'm having so much fun getting all my candy ready for the trick-or-treaters. I bought several hundred bags. I limited myself to just my favorite kinds. I had to sample a few from each bag so I could make sure that the candy was tasty. [Snort, snort.] Excuse me. Now, I'm going to go and put my treats in a nice big bowl.

[Exit Piggy Rae, enter Big Bad Wolf.]

BIG BAD WOLF: Hello, boys and girls. I am the Big Bad Wolf. Very, very, very big and very, very, very bad. Oh my, I am so hungry for some delicious roasted pig! I watched a clever little pig build a house down the street. One day I went down there and I knocked on her door, [Make knocking sound.] and I said,

"Little pig, little pig, let me come in!"

[Audience repeats:] "Little pig, little pig, let me come in!"

[If the audience needs prompting, do so here.]

Then I huffed and puffed, but it was a very strong house—built with brick. I blew myself silly that day, but could not blooooowwww the house down.

I wonder how I can outsmart her? Hmm, . . . I don't know what to do; she is such a clever little pig.

Gosh! I'm so hungry. What can I do, what can I do?

Wait! Hold everything! It's Halloween night, so all I need to do is knock on her door say, "Trick or Treat!" Then she will open her door. Why didn't I think of it before?

I'll go right now.

[For the following sequence, only the puppet that is speaking appears on stage.]

PIGGY RAE: [Sing to the tune of "Three Blind Mice."]

Three black cats, three black cats,

Chasing rats, chasing rats,

All of them having tons of fun

Pouncing and jumping as they run,

On Halloween, on Halloween!

[Make knocking sound.]

Oh my, one of my little trick-or-treaters has arrived! I wonder what cute costume I will see.

BIG BAD WOLF: [Make another knocking sound.] Little pig, little pig let me come in!

[Audience repeats:] "Little pig, little pig, let me come in!"

PIGGY RAE: Look at that cute little wolf. He is just adorable! [Asks audience.] Do you think that I should let him come in?

[Allow audience to tell her not to let him in.]

Oh my! I see what you mean. He is not very adorable. He is pretty scary. I think he is the Big Bad Wolf who lives down the street, and he is trying to trick me, the Clever Little Pig. If I let him in, he's going to roast me for sure!

[Make another knocking sound.]

You can't fool me. You are the Big Bad Wolf, and you cannot come in. Not by the hair on my chinny-chin-chin!

[Audience repeats:] "Not by the hair on my chinny-chin-chin!"

BIG BAD WOLF: [To audience.] I told you that she is a very clever pig. Perhaps this calls for more drastic measures. I have another idea. Because today is Halloween, if I put on a costume, she will not recognize me. I must go back home and find a costume. I know! I will dress up like a pirate, and I will fool the Clever Little Pig into letting me in. As they say on the South Seas, "Whar be the wharf?"

PIGGY RAE: Oh, y'all, that was such a close call. I must be very careful, and clever, as usual.

[Exit Piggy Rae, put eye patch on Big Bad Wolf.]

[Enter Big Bad Wolf wearing eye patch.]

BIG BAD WOLF: Shiver me timbers. This hat and eye patch will fool everybody. I look just like a pirate. The Clever Little Pig will never guess that it is I, the Big Bad Wolf! Weigh anchor me hearty. A storm's a-brewing. Arrrrgh! And now it's time for me to hoist sail and go get me a tasty pig varmint to roast for my dinner. I have a fierce fire in me belly!

PIGGY RAE: I love Halloween. I love all the cute costumes. I especially love all the candy. [Snort, snort.] Excuse me. I can hardly wait for someone to knock on my door.

BIG BAD WOLF: Shhh! Do not tell the Clever Little Pig about my excellent disguise!

[Make knocking sound.]

PIGGY RAE: Oh, I'm very excited to give a yummy treat to this Halloweener.

BIG BAD WOLF: [Make knocking sound.]

"Little pig, little pig, let me come in!"

[Audience repeats:] "Little pig, little pig, let me come in!"

PIGGY RAE: Hold everything! That sounds like the Big Bad Wolf again!

BIG BAD WOLF: I meant to say, "Bring me a noggin of treats for Halloween now, won't you matey?"

PIGGY RAE: Oh, silly me! I'm getting paranoid! Paranoid means that I'm afraid for no reason at all. Because, all I see is a cute little fellow dressed up like a pirate! [To audience.] Do you think it is a trick-or-treater in a pirate costume? Should I let him in?

[Allow time for audience to respond.]

Oh, I see what you mean. He sounds like the Big Bad Wolf and he sort of looks like the Big Bad Wolf!

[Make another knocking sound.]

It might be Halloween, but you can't trick me! You're the Big Bad Wolf! I am the Clever Little Pig. I will not let you in, not by the hair on my chinny-chin-chin.

[Audience repeats:] "Not by the hair on my chinny-chin-chin!"

BIG BAD WOLF: Oh, Skuttle me skippers! I'm a pirate!

PIGGY RAE: You are the Big Bad Wolf, and you want to roast me for dinner! I will not let you in! Not by the hair on my chinny-chin-chin!

[Audience repeats:] "Not by the hair on my chinny-chin-chin!"

BIG BAD WOLF: Well, blow me down! Rats! I need a better costume to trick that Clever Little Pig! I'll have to think of a very good costume. A disguise that will fool everyone! Aha! I have the perfect idea!

[Wolf exits. No puppets are on stage. Place wig on Big Bad Wolf while singing the following song.]

BIG BAD WOLF: [Singing offstage to the tune of "Clementine."]

I feel pretty, I feel pretty.

I will fool the Clever Pig.

I look nice and very tricky,

I will fool the Clever Pig.

[Enters wearing blond wig.] What do you think of this costume? My blond wig will fool everybody. I look just like a pretty little girl. This Clever Little Pig will never guess that it is I, the Big Bad Wolf. I will go to her house and try again. This time I think I will outwit her. [Wolf exits. Piggy Rae enters.]

PIGGY RAE: [Sings to the tune of "Clementine."]

I like candy, I like candy.

I like chocolate, I like cream.

I like candy, I like candy.

Eating candy is my dream!

It is a good thing that I am such a clever little pig. Otherwise I might be sitting in a roasting pan right now. I must be on the lookout for the Big Bad Wolf in case he comes back.

BIG BAD WOLF: Shhhh! Do not tell the Clever Little Pig about my costume!

[Make knocking sound.]

PIGGY RAE: Oh, finally! I have a trick-or-treater. Oh, look, it's a pretty little girl! I'll give her a piece of yummy candy.

BIG BAD WOLF: [Make another knocking sound.] Little pig, little pig, let me come in.

[Audience repeats:] "Little pig, little pig, let me come in!"

PIGGY RAE: Hold everything! That is not a little girl. That sounds like the Big Bad Wolf!

BIG BAD WOLF: [Using a sugary sweet, high-pitched voice.] Oopsie Daisy, what I really meant to say was, "Trick or Treat! Don't you have a small piece of candy for me, a pretty little girl?"

PIGGY RAE: [To audience.] There I go being paranoid again! Do you remember what paranoid means? [Pause for audience to respond.] That's right; it means being scared for no reason at all.

Look—it's only a pretty little girl! Do you think I should let her in?

[Allow time for audience to respond.]

Oh, I see what you mean. She has such big ears and such big eyes and such big sharp teeth! [Make another knocking sound.] Oh, my! You're not a pretty little girl OR a trick-or-treater! You are the Big Bad Wolf! And you cannot come into my house, not by the hair on my chinny-chin-chin.

[Audience repeats:] "Not by the hair on my chinny-chin-chin!"

BIG BAD WOLF: Oh, rats! I give up! I was very hungry and I tried to trick you. But you are the Clever Little Pig and I cannot fool you, even with my excellent Halloween costumes. I'm sorry for trying to trick you.

PIGGY RAE: You should be sorry. We are neighbors, and we should try to get along. You know what? I'm hungry, too. While I was waiting for the trick-or-treaters to come to my house, I accidentally ate several bags of candy. [Snort, snort.] Excuse me. You know you're not supposed to eat candy before dinner. Now I have a sugar slump. I need something substantial to eat for dinner.

BIG BAD WOLF: Do you like pizza? We could go down to the neighborhood pizza restaurant.

PIGGY RAE: Did you say pizza? Pizza is my favorite food! I love pizza!

BIG BAD WOLF: Well, we could be friends and go have a pizza together. As you say, we are neighbors. Besides, I would like to be friends with a clever little pig like you.

PIGGY RAE: I can be your friend. Do you promise not to roast me?

BIG BAD WOLF: I promise. No more pig for me!

PIGGY RAE: Okay, let's go get some pizza. I'm starving!

[Both puppets exit. Brief pause. Place both puppets back on the stage. They sing to the tune of "Here We Go 'round the Mulberry Bush.":]

PIGGY RAE: I am friends with the Big Bad Wolf,

The Big Bad Wolf,

The Big Bad Wolf.

BIG BAD WOLF: I am friends with Piggy Rae

The Clever Little Pig!

[Exit Piggy Rae and the Big Bad Wolf.]

[Enter Alistair McMoose.]

ALISTAIR McMOOSE: And that brings us to a conclusion of another *Moosterpiece Theater*—way, way, way off Broadway theater. Completely ridiculous!

But I must admit, I was quite fooled by the first-rate costumes that the Big Bad Wolf was wearing. Good thing the Clever Little Pig had you folks here to keep her on her toes!

And now I bid you all adieu! Happy Halloween!

The End

LITERACY TO GO

Dear Parents and Caregivers,

"The Three Little Pigs" remains a timeless tale. Today we performed a puppet show featuring Piggy Rae as the third little pig, the one who cleverly outsmarted the Big Bad Wolf. We asked you to repeat two different phrases during our puppet show: "Little pig, little pig, let me come in," and "Not by the hair on my chinny-chin-chin!"

The repetition of text is a technique that helps to teach phonological awareness, as it helps children become used to hearing and saying the sounds of the words we use in our language. The booklist below offers titles that have repetitive text as an integral part of the book. When reading these books to your child, use your finger to follow along with the repeating refrain. This helps introduce the early literacy skill of print awareness, or noticing print.

You and your child will have fun reading these books together.

Literacy To Go Take Home Menu

Books that build phonological awareness through repetitive text: The following books have a refrain that is repeated throughout. Encourage your child to say the refrain with you or repeat after you when reading these books together.

Anderson, Peggy Perry. *Joe on the Go*.
Joe wants to play and finally finds someone who will play with him: Grandma.

Aylesworth, Jim. *Little Bitty Mousie*.
A mouse sniffs her way through the alphabet.

Emberley, Ed. *Go Away, Big Green Monster!*
Strategically cut out pages make this fun story an adventurous page-turner.

Fleming, Denise. *The Cow Who Clucked*.
A cow is looking for her moo, but, "It is not you who has my moo!" Where will she find it?

Gerritsen, Paula. *Nuts*.
A minimal amount of text is used to describe a tiny mouse gathering nuts for the winter.

Gerstein, Mordicai. *Leaving the Nest*.
A bevy of backyard animals watch a baby blue jay take flight.

Harper, Anita. *It's Not Fair!*
It's not fair that baby brother gets away with so much. It's not fair that big sister gets to do so much.

Hennessy, B[arbara] G. *The Boy Who Cried Wolf*.
One of Aesop's fables, retold with descriptive words, wonderful illustrations, and a strong lesson.

Martin, Bill, Jr. *Brown Bear, Brown Bear What Do You See?*
A modern classic.

Mayr, Diane. *Run, Turkey, Run*.
It is Thanksgiving time, and the turkey better "run, turkey, run!"

Meyers, Susan. *Kittens! Kittens! Kittens!* and *Puppies! Puppies! Puppies!*
Easy to read yet descriptive, the title is repeated throughout each book.

Parker, Marjorie Blain. *Your Kind of Mommy*.
Animal mommies and people mommies love their babies.

Rosen, Michael. *Bear's Day Out.*
Many repeatable refrains are used to describe Bear's adventure from a cave to the city.

Scieszka, Jon. [with help from David Shannon, Loren Long, and David Gordon]. *Smash! Crash!*
There will be no stopping the children from repeating "Smash! Crash!"

Shannon, David. *Good Boy, Fergus!*
Fergus is not the most well-behaved dog, but he's certainly cute.

Shapiro, Jody Fickes. *Family Lullaby.*
Parents, grandparents, everyone loves baby.

Sherry, Kevin. *I'm the Biggest Thing in the Ocean.*
A giant squid thinks he is the biggest thing in the ocean.

Shulevitz, Uri. *So Sleepy Story.*
Everything in the house is "so sleepy."

Sillifant, Alec. *Farmer Ham.*
Farmer Ham can't seem to scare away crows.

Squires, Janet. *The Gingerbread Cowboy.*
"Giddy-up, giddy-up as fast as you can. You can't catch me; I'm the Gingerbread Man."

Stainton, Sue. *I Love Cats.*
If you love cats, you'll love this book.

Stoeke, Janet Morgan. *The Bus Stop.*
A school bus ride instills confidence in children.

Tafuri, Nancy. *The Busy Little Squirrel.*
A busy squirrel gathers food for the winter.

Weaver, Tess. *Cat Jumped In!*
Cat jumps in through a window, into a closet, where next?

Wilson, Karma. *Bear Snores On.*
Bear hibernates and nothing (maybe) wakes him up.

Wilson, Karma. *Bear Wants More.*
The bear from *Bear Snores On* wakes up from his hibernation, and he is hungry!

Wilson, Karma. *Princess Me.*
Perfect read-aloud for princesses.

Wood, Audrey. *King Bidgood's in the Bathtub.*
Will anyone be able to figure out how to get the king out of the tub? Because he won't get out!

Wood, Audrey. *Silly Sally.*
You'll sing along with this silly story.

Zimmerman, Andrea Griffing. *Dig!*
A counting rhyme at a construction site.

You're Invited to a
PUPPET SHOW!
Come to storytime and a special puppet show performance of

MOOSTERPIECE THEATER: CLEVER PIGGY RAE AND THE BIG BAD WOLF

The Big Bad Wolf puts on different Halloween costumes to try to fool Piggy Rae into opening the door and letting him come in. With the help of the audience, Clever Piggy Rae cannot be tricked.

Our puppet show is specially designed for children ages three through eight and their parents, and will help build phonological awareness, an important literacy skill.

Date (and day of week): _____

At (library name & address, room number or area)

_____

Is Piggy Rae Afraid of the Big Bad Wolf?

From *Puppet Plays Plus: Using Stock Characters to Entertain and Teach Early Literacy* by Laurel L. Iakovakis. Westport, CT: Libraries Unlimited. Copyright © 2009.

Making an Eye Patch

Materials needed:

      10-inch square of black felt

      15-inch piece of ¼-inch wide black elastic

Cut a piece of black felt large enough to cover the eye of the wolf puppet you are using. Fold down the top portion and stitch it down, leaving an opening to slide through a piece of ¼-inch black elastic. Cut a strip of ¼-inch black elastic long enough to fit around the head of the wolf puppet you are using. Thread the elastic through the opening in the felt. Size it to the head of the wolf puppet, and tie the elastic. Slip it over the wolf's head when needed.

Making a Blond Wig

Materials needed:

      Skein of yellow yarn

      Hair bow (optional)

      Hot glue and glue gun

To create the long hair, cut 30 pieces of yellow yarn, each 30 inches long. Lay flat, side by side. Cut two 6-inch pieces of yellow yarn. Tie them gently through the center of the laid out yarn. You now have 15 inches of yarn on each side of the knots. Use hot glue to reinforce along both sides of the knotted yarn.

To create the bangs for the wig, cut 10 pieces of yellow yarn, each 10 inches long.

Lay flat, side by side. Cut a 6-inch piece of yellow yarn. Tie it through the center of the 10-inch pieces of yarn. You now have 5 inches of yarn on each side of the knot. Use hot glue to reinforce along both sides of the knotted yarn.

To construct the wig, place the 5-inch segments on top of the knots on the 15-inch segments. Hang the shorter segments in front so they look like bangs. Hot glue the underside so all the segments stay in place. Trim any straggly ends. Attach the hair bow, if using.

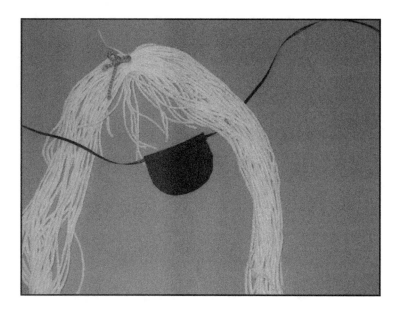

MOOSTERPIECE THEATER: PIGGY RAE-ELLA

Related Themes: Fairy tales, "Cinderella" stories, Princesses, Magic

Overview: This storytime focuses on a reenactment of a scene from the classic, favorite tale "Cinderella." In the puppet play, Alistair McMoose introduces the *Moosterpiece Theater* version of "Cinderella." Granny, as Granny Godmother, uses magic to help Piggy Rae, starring as Piggy Rae-ella, find just the right outfit to wear to the ball.

Through the retelling of this scene, the early literacy focus of the storytime is the narrative skill.

Early Literacy Skill Focus: This show and theme focus on *narrative skills*—telling stories. Audience participation helps "conjure-up" some magic words for Granny to use to help Piggy Rae-ella obtain the right outfit for the ball.

The Literacy To Go take home menu suggests various "Cinderella" stories to read at home and other titles that beg to be read and retold.

Other Literacy Opportunities:

- **Vocabulary:** Before the puppet show, talk about the following vocabulary words, which are used in the puppet show. Ask what these words mean.

    - *Ridiculous*: silly, absurd
    - *Ingénue*: pretty young heroine
    - *Tiara*: flashy crown
    - *Salary*: money earned at work
    - *Limousine*: fancy long car driven by a chauffeur for special occasions.

- **Print awareness:** An additional literacy skill you can promote with this program is print awareness. After the puppet show, write some of the magic words that were used in the course of the puppet show on an easel or wipe-off board. Ask the audience to help you remember. Then use your finger to follow the print as you repeat the words aloud.

- **Narrative skills:** Telling stories through sharing exemplary children's literature is one of the traditional goals of storytime. Serve as a role model for parents and caregivers by retelling selected literature. Use descriptive vocabulary and give your synopsis a beginning, middle, and end.

    Choose one of the read-aloud stories to tell or retell the puppet show after you have performed it. Embellish the storytelling by asking open-ended questions such as, "What do you think happens next?" "How does Piggy Rae-ella get to the ball?" "What do you think Piggy Rae-ella loses at the stroke of midnight?"

    These techniques set an example for how parents and caregivers can encourage storytelling and build narrative skills at home.

Materials Needed:

- Puppets: Alistair McMoose, Piggy Rae, Granny.

- Props: Dirty white shawl for Piggy Rae to wear, bell that rings, small wand, bread pan, colorful sock to fit over the snout of Piggy Rae, Groucho Marx glasses with nose and moustache, fisherman hat with hooks and lures.

- Princess items for display table: wands, tiaras, etc.

- Literacy To Go handouts for participants (see pp. 95–96).

- Promotional flyers (see p. 97).

- Display books for checkout; use titles provided on Literacy To Go handout.

- Titles for read-alouds.

Preparation:

A few weeks or more before the program

- Decide on your program theme.
- Announce the storytime program in the library Web site and newsletter.
- Reproduce the promotional flyer (p. 97), and distribute copies to caregivers at the library.

A week or two before the program

- Select and gather your read-aloud titles, as well as display books for checkout, puppets, and props.
- Make Piggy Rae's dirty white shawl: Cut a piece of muslin and stain it with brown, black, and grey permanent markers.
- Collect the princess objects for the Literacy To Go display.
- Reproduce the Literacy To Go materials (see pp. 95–96).
- Practice the read-aloud books and the puppet play.

On the day of the program

- Create a display of checkout material based on the narrative skill theme of stories that offer opportunities to be retold.
- Decorate your display with princess items.
- Set up the easel or wipe-off board to write the magic words (after the puppet show) to support print awareness.

Puppet Show Performance Tips: Feel free to embellish Piggy Rae's attire with items of local interest. Librarians in the Southwest may want to use a red chili necklace; in Wisconsin, a Cheese-head hat would be funny; use a cowboy hat in cowboy country, etc. Perhaps you would like to use a baseball cap or football helmet from a local sports team.

If you need two hands to change Piggy Rae's clothes, have Granny exit the stage while saying, "I'm going to go see what's keeping her," or, "Where is that girl?"

It is difficult to have Granny Godmother hold the magic wand throughout the show. Try wrapping a rubber band around the wand and Granny's hand to keep the wand in place.

Someone from the audience may suggest using the magic word "please" before you are ready to do so. Choose any words from the list below, but don't use *please* until it is time.

Here is a list of magic words, in case the audience needs prompting:

> *Abracadabra*
>
> *Presto-chango*
>
> *Bippity-boppity-boo*
>
> *Peanut butter and jelly*
>
> *Macaroni and cheese*
>
> *Shazam*
>
> *Criss-cross applesauce*
>
> *Alakazam*
>
> *Hocus pocus*

The Program

During the read-aloud segment: After welcoming participants, gather children and caregivers into a semicircle around your storytelling chair. After reading some of your selected literature, retell a story to set the example of how caregivers can teach the narrative skill at home.

Talk about Cinderella's makeover to get ready for the ball. Tell them that a Fairy Godmother grants Cinderella's wish to go to the ball. She dresses her in a beautiful outfit and provides a ride for her in a handsome coach. Talking about this will help to prepare the children for the puppet show.

Introduce the puppet show: Have the group assemble comfortably around the puppet stage. As leader, address the group with the following welcome.

> Around the world there are many versions of the "Cinderella" tale. Today's puppet show features the famous Piggy Rae, whom we call Piggy Rae-ella. Granny, as Granny Godmother, helps Piggy Rae-ella get dressed for the ball. However, as usual in *Moosterpiece Theater*, things go wrong. Granny Godmother needs your help. Think hard about some good magic words that might help Granny Godmother get Piggy Rae-ella dressed. We'll also need you to help Piggy Rae-ella decide if the outfits that Granny selects are the best clothes to wear to the ball. Get ready, now, for Alistair McMoose to introduce the puppet show.

Move to your place behind the puppet stage to begin the show.

After the puppet show: Ask the audience what they think happens next. Prompt with questions such as, "How do you think Piggy Rae got to the ball?" Use some of the open-ended questions listed above. Ask, "When has using the magic word *please* ever helped you to get something?"

Talk about the vocabulary words listed above.

If you have time, write the magic words used in the puppet show on an easel or wipe-off board. This idea is described under the "print awareness" heading.

Older children can be introduced to the differences in "Cinderella" stories based on culture, ethnicity, and regions of the world. Parents may want to talk more about this at home.

Hand out copies of the Literacy To Go sheets to caregivers, explaining that it offers narrative skill tips to use at home. Encourage caregivers to check out the "Cinderella" stories and other books that support narrative skills.

Have the puppets tell the children good-bye.

MOOSTERPIECE THEATER: PIGGY RAE-ELLA

Puppets:

    Alistair McMoose

    Piggy Rae

    Granny

Props:

    Dirty white shawl

    Bell that rings (not seen by audience)

    Small wand

    Bread pan to fit over Piggy Rae's head

    Colorful sock to fit over Piggy Rae's snout

    Groucho Marx glasses with nose and moustache

    Fisherman hat with bait, hooks, and lures

    Piggy Rae's pink feather boa

[Enter Alistair McMoose.]

ALISTAIR McMOOSE: Good morning, boys and girls, ladies and gentlemen. I am Alistair McMoose, host of Moosterpiece Theater: way, way, way off Broadway theater. Prepare for a silly plot, horrendous acting, and a completely ridiculous ending. Boys and girls, do you know what *ridiculous* means? [Pause for audience to respond.] That's right. It means totally, entirely, extremely silly! Ridiculous—it's a fun word to say.

What kind of ending does this play have? [Pause for audience to respond.] Yes. It has a ridiculous ending.

However, as luck would have it, we are fortunate that our favorite ingénue, superstar Piggy Rae, will be here to star in our production of "Piggy Rae-ella," a silly version of "Cinderella."

From *Puppet Plays Plus: Using Stock Characters to Entertain and Teach Early Literacy* by Laurel L. Iakovakis.
Westport, CT: Libraries Unlimited. Copyright © 2009.

PIGGY RAE:	Hi, y'all! Hi, hi, hi! It is I, Piggy Rae. Aren't you lucky that I was able to make some space in my busy schedule to come and perform for you today? You people are the luckiest folks in the world. Just wait until you see me in my beautiful ball gown being driven in a pumpkin coach by a team of white horses. I, in my glass slippers and diamond tiara . . . .
ALISTAIR McMOOSE:	Piggy Rae! Hold on just a moment. First of all, I am the host of Moosterpiece Theater, and I get to do the introductions. You simply must learn to wait your turn and remain offstage until I am finished.
PIGGY RAE:	Oh yeah, right. I think you mentioned that once before.
ALISTAIR McMOOSE:	Actually, I mention it on every episode of Moosterpiece Theater.
PIGGY RAE:	It's not my fault if my fans are anxious to see me.
ALISTAIR McMOOSE:	But wait, as long as you are here, I've got some other news for you.
PIGGY RAE:	Ohhhh . . . I'm excited! What's the news? Some juicy gossip?
ALISTAIR McMOOSE:	No, no, Piggy Rae. None of that. As you know, Moosterpiece Theater is renowned for being skimpy.
PIGGY RAE:	Skimpy?
ALISTAIR McMOOSE:	Cheap. We don't spend very much money.
PIGGY RAE:	So I've heard. Except for my salary, of course, which is extremely high.
ALISTAIR McMOOSE:	Today's performance of "Cinderella" will not feature any white horses or a pumpkin coach.
PIGGY RAE:	Really?
ALISTAIR McMOOSE:	Nor will there be any beautiful ball gown or glass slippers, and most assuredly no diamond tiara.
PIGGY RAE:	What??? How can I be Cinderella without the fancy dress and extravagant ride to the ball? And no glass slippers? What's with that?

ALISTAIR McMOOSE: It was necessary to make some budgetary adjustments.

PIGGY RAE: This will be quite a stretch for even as fabulous an actress as I, Piggy Rae.

ALISTAIR McMOOSE: Well, now you know. Please wait backstage until I've given you a proper introduction.

[Piggy Rae exits.]

Yes, as I was saying . . . .

Today's performance will star Piggy Rae, famous way, way, way off Broadway actress, in "Piggy Rae-ella," the Moosterpiece Theater version of the classic "Cinderella." Many of you will fondly remember the year 2001, when she was crowned Miss Pork Rind. And now I present Piggy Rae in her own fairy tale, "Piggy Rae-ella." Let's give her a nice warm welcome.

[Alistair exits. Piggy Rae enters without her pink feather boa. She is wearing a dirty white shawl tied around her neck.]

PIGGY RAE: Oh, woe is me, Piggy Rae-ella. I work all day, cleaning and cooking. Of course underneath all this dirt, I am gorgeous. I live with my hideous, mean, and ugly stepsisters and stepmother, who make me do all the dirty work. Oh, woe is me, Piggy Rae-ella.

And tonight is the grand ball. All the ladies in the countryside have been invited. The handsome prince will be looking for a wife to become his princess. Alas, I cannot go because I'm a mess what with all this cleaning. Oh woe is me, Piggy Rae-ella.

I wish I had a fairy godmother who could make me a new outfit.

[Ring bell. Pause.]

What could that be?

[Granny enters, carrying a small wand.]

Are you my fairy godmother?

GRANNY: No, Piggy Rae. It's just me, Granny.

PIGGY RAE: Granny, we are acting. You're supposed to be pretending to be my fairy godmother.

GRANNY: Oh yeah, that's right. Alistair went over all this with me . . . sorry. Let's do that part again. [She exits.]

PIGGY RAE: [To audience.] Sorry about that, girls and boys. Granny doesn't have the way, way, way off Broadway acting experience that I do.

I wish I had a fairy godmother who could make me a new outfit.

[Ring bell. Pause.]

What could that be?

[Granny enters, carrying a small wand.]

Are you my fairy godmother?

GRANNY: Yes. But, Piggy Rae, please call me Granny.

PIGGY RAE: Granny! Come on! You have to pretend.

GRANNY: Okay then, call me Granny Godmother.

PIGGY RAE: Fine. But don't call me Piggy Rae. Call me Piggy Rae-ella.

GRANNY: That's an adorable name, Piggy Rae. I mean Piggy Rae-ella.

PIGGY RAE: Thank you. Now, I have to get back into character.

Oh my! Look, y'all! It's my very own Granny Godmother. I was just wishing for a new outfit to wear to the ball so that I can dance with the prince. Then he will fall in love with me. And search the kingdom to find me.

GRANNY: I have my magic wand, so I can do anything. Just step behind that curtain, and we will transform you into a thing of beauty.

[Piggy Rae exits.]

PIGGY RAE: [Offstage.] I'm ready for my new outfit, Granny Godmother!

GRANNY: [Waves wand.] Okay, let's see your outfit.

PIGGY RAE: [Offstage.] Nothing happened. I still look the same. I think that you have to say some magic words.

GRANNY: Oh yeah, that's right. Let's see. I'll say open sesame!

[Granny waves the wand. Piggy Rae reenters wearing a bread pan on her head.]

PIGGY RAE: How do I look? Am I gorgeous in my new outfit?

GRANNY: Hmmm, . . . I'm not sure. What do you think, boys and girls? Should Piggy Rae-ella wear this to the ball?

[Allow the audience to say no.]

PIGGY RAE: Granny Godmother, I think they're right. I don't think that I should wear a bread pan on my head to meet my new boyfriend.

GRANNY: Perhaps we should try again.

PIGGY RAE: Yeah, use some better magic words this time. [She exits.]

GRANNY: Boys and girls, can you help me think up some magic words? Let's see, we could try presto-chango. What do you think of that?

[Use a suggestion from the audience, or use presto-chango. Granny waves the wand.]

C'mon, Piggy Rae-ella! I want to see your new outfit!

PIGGY RAE: [Reenters with a colorful sock around her snout, which causes her to mumble or to talk as if with a stuffy nose.] Something tells me that I should not wear this to the ball. Do y'all think I look pretty?

[Allow time for audience to respond.]

GRANNY: That looks sillier than a bread pan.

PIGGY RAE: [Still mumbling.] You can say that again!

GRANNY: How's that? I can't understand you. If you're going to be a princess, Piggy Rae-ella, you need to speak clearly.

PIGGY RAE: [Mumbling.] I cannot talk very well when I have a sock around my snout!

GRANNY: You better go behind the curtain and let me try again.

[Piggy Rae exits.]

Boys and girls, we need better magic words. Who knows some good magic words?

[Allow time for audience to respond.]

[Using a magic word suggestion from the audience and waving wand.] Piggy Rae-ella, where are you?

PIGGY RAE: [Reenters wearing Groucho Marx glasses with nose and moustache.] Finally! I'm beautiful! This is what I shall wear to the ball!

GRANNY: [Screams!] What did you do to Piggy Rae-ella? Where is she? [Calls behind curtain.]

Piggy Rae-ella! Piggy Rae-ella!

PIGGY RAE: Granny Godmother. I'm right here. It is I, Piggy Rae-ella. Am I so beautiful that you don't recognize me?

GRANNY: I wouldn't exactly call you beautiful.

PIGGY RAE: Oh? Am I pretty?

GRANNY: Not pretty either.

PIGGY RAE: Gorgeous?

GRANNY: Not quite. What's the opposite of gorgeous?

PIGGY RAE: Ridiculous?

GRANNY: That's about right.

PIGGY RAE: I look ridiculous?

GRANNY: Boys and girls, do you think Piggy Rae should wear this to the ball?

[Allow time for audience to respond.]

Sorry, Piggy Rae-ella. The boys and girls think that you look ridiculous, too. Tell you what, let's give it another try. I know I've got some magic in me somewhere. It's probably this magic wand. I'm not too sure it works.

PIGGY RAE: Well, it's doing something, just not the right thing. We better get this figured out, y'all, or I won't get to go to the ball. And I won't get to dance with the handsome prince, and then he won't have the chance to fall in love with me. Oh, woe is me, Piggy-Rae-ella

GRANNY: You skedaddle behind that curtain. We've got to try again. [To audience.] Boys and girls, I need your help. Let's try this. Everyone shout out every magic word you can think of. I'll count to three and then we shout out some magic words. One, two, three . . .

[Allow time for audience to respond. Granny may shout out words, too.]

That should do it! Come here, Piggy Rae-ella; let's see if this is the proper ballroom attire!

PIGGY RAE: [Reenters wearing a fisherman hat with lures, bait, and fish hooks hanging on it.] How do I look?

GRANNY: I think you look perfect if you are going to go fishing.

PIGGY RAE: Oh, Granny Godmother! I think it's going to be midnight before I get the right outfit and get to go meet the handsome prince. The ball will be over and I'll still be here, and you'll still be waving that wand around. I'll never find anything pretty to wear. I want to meet my handsome prince!

GRANNY: Boys and girls, we need some mighty powerful magic words this time. Who knows some really powerful words?

[Allow time for audience to respond.]

Those are some mighty fine magic words.

PIGGY RAE: Y'all, PLEASE! I need some help with this one.

GRANNY: Piggy Rae-ella, what did you say?

PIGGY RAE: I said, "Please help."

GRANNY: Well, I'll be! I think that's the answer. I know that I'm always reminding my sweet little grandson, Bernie Bear, to "Say the magic word."

PIGGY RAE: We should say "Please!"

GRANNY: Exactly!

PIGGY RAE: Hmmm. Y'all, I think Granny Godmother is on to something here. I'll go behind the curtain, and y'all say please.

GRANNY: Okay, at the count of five, let's say please. One, two, three, four, five . . . .

[Allow the audience to say "Please."]

Piggy Rae-ella, come on down!

PIGGY RAE: [Reenters wearing her pink feather boa.] Now I really feel pretty and special.

GRANNY: It's your pink feather boa! You are gorgeous! Piggy Rae-ella, you always look fabulous in pink. Boys and girls, don't you think Piggy Rae-ella is gorgeous and that the handsome prince will fall in love with her?

[Allow time for audience to respond.]

I agree! Now Piggy Rae-ella, you give Granny Godmother a big hug and head on off to the ball.

PIGGY RAE: And I have another magic word, myself! It's "Thank you!" And now I'm off to dance the night away!

GRANNY: Be sure to leave the ball at the stroke of midnight! Have fun, Piggy Rae-ella!

PIGGY RAE: Wait! How am I going to get to the ball?

GRANNY: Oh dear, I hadn't thought of that. I guess you'll have to walk.

PIGGY RAE: Hold it! That's not happening; I'm not going to walk. Do you think you can whip up a fancy limousine with that wand of yours, Granny Godmother?

GRANNY: I suppose I can try. We better head outside and I'll start up with the wand waving and the magic words again.

PIGGY RAE: Let's hurry!

[Granny and Piggy Rae exit.]

ALISTAIR McMOOSE: And that, ladies and gentlemen, boys and girls, brings to a conclusion another episode of Moosterpiece Theater: way, way, way off Broadway theater. I hope you were all properly enchanted. There might still be time for me to get to the ball and perhaps have a dance with Piggy Rae-ella. And now, I bid you all adieu.

The End

LITERACY TO GO

Dear Parents and Caregivers,

Choose some books from the list below to read aloud to your child. Allow him or her to retell you any part of it in his or her own words. Telling stories is an important early literacy skill, called narrative skills. After your child retells the story, add some descriptive words of your own to help build vocabulary. The following list begins with some "Cinderella" stories and concludes with other stories that follow a sequence of events and beg to be retold.

On your way home from storytime today, see how many funny pieces of clothing you and your child can remember Piggy Rae putting on before she found the best one to wear.

See you next week!

Literacy To Go Take Home Menu

Books that build narrative skills: Reading these "Cinderella" stories from around the world will present opportunities for storytelling. Embellish upon the segment of the "Cinderella" story told in the puppet show. The second list contains other recommended children's literature that offers opportunities for reading and retelling.

Climo, Shirley. *The Korean Cinderella.*
Delight in the accomplishments of Pear Blossom.

Compton, Joanne Ward. *Ashpet: An Appalachian Tale.*
Instead of a fancy dress ball, this Cinderella story takes place at a "church meetin' " and the handsome prince is the doctor's son.

Craft, K. Y. *Cinderella.*
Lavish illustrations reminiscent of seventeenth-century French art.

dePaola, Tomie. *Adelita: A Mexican Cinderella Story.*
This story uses some Spanish text that is translated within the work.

Ehrlich, Amy. *Cinderella.*
Renowned for its beautiful illustrations by Susan Jeffers.

Fleischman, Paul. *Glass Slipper, Gold Sandal : A Worldwide Cinderella.*
Combines multiple cultural retellings of "Cinderella" in one story.

Goode, Diane. *Cinderella, the Dog and Her Little Glass Slipper.*
This version has dogs instead of people.

Hayes, Joe. *Little Gold Star: a Cinderella Story. Estrellita de Oro: A Cinderella Cuento.* Retold in Spanish & English.
A bright gold star glows brightly on Arcía's forehead and attracts the attention of the prince.

Hickox, Rebecca. *The Golden Sandal: A Middle Eastern Cinderella.*
A magical fish and a delicate gold sandal are a part of this Middle Eastern version of "Cinderella."

Hill, Margaret Bateson. *Chanda and the Mirror of Moonlight.*
The story takes place in India and is written in both English and Hindi.

Marineau, Michèle. *Cinderella.*
A modern interpretation of "Cinderella" features a gal who takes charge of her own life and goes to the ball in a sports car and pointy-toed shoes.

From *Puppet Plays Plus: Using Stock Characters to Entertain and Teach Early Literacy* by Laurel L. Iakovakis. Westport, CT: Libraries Unlimited. Copyright © 2009.

Perlman, Janet. *Cinderella Penguin: Or, The Little Glass Flipper.*
> A delightful variation with penguins.

San Souci, Daniel. *Sootface: An Ojibwa Cinderella Story.*
> An Ojibwa tale, very similar to *The Rough-Face Girl* by Rafe Martin.

Young, Amy. *Belinda and the Glass Slipper.*
> This version is for ballet lovers.

Other stories that build narrative skills: Read these books aloud and share in retelling them.

Denise, Anika. *Pigs Love Potatoes.*
> A counting and rhyming book. Who stops by mama's house and wants to eat potatoes?

Ehrlich, Amy. *The Random House Book of Fairy Tales.*
> A collection of much-loved fairy tales.

Garland, Michael. *How Many Mice?*
> Succinct sentences advance the plot. Also introduces numbers and math.

Inches, Alison. *The Stuffed Animals Get Ready for Bed.*
> A little girl patiently prepares her naughty stuffed animals for bedtime.

Krensky, Stephen. *Big Bad Wolves at School.*
> A nature-loving wolf goes to big bad wolf school to learn to huff and puff.

LaRochelle, David. *The End.*
> This fairy tale is told in reverse—it begins with "They lived happily ever after." An innovative storytelling technique.

Lester, Helen. *Tacky the Penguin.*
> A penguin who has his own way of doing things saves his friends.

Murphy, Jill. *Mr. Large in Charge.*
> When Mrs. Large, an elephant, has to spend the day sick in bed, Mr. Large takes over running the household.

Ohi, Ruth. *Me and My Brother.*
> Story of two brothers and how they play.

Plourde, Lynn. *A Mountain of Mittens.*
> After reading this book, try to remember how many ways the main character lost her mittens.

Shulman, Lisa. *Over in the Meadow at the Big Ballet.*
> Review all the steps necessary to put on a dance recital.

Thompson, Lauren. *Little Quack.*
> A hesitant duck gets ready for a swim.

Weninger, Brigitte. *Bye-bye, Binky.*
> You'll enjoy talking about this story of a kitten who is ready to give up her pacifier.

You're Invited to a
PUPPET SHOW!
Come to storytime and a special puppet show performance of

MOOSTERPIECE THEATER: PIGGY RAE-ELLA

Come and enjoy our silly version of "Cinderella," as Granny Godmother tries to help Piggy Rae-ella dress up for the ball. What will Piggy Rae-ella wear? Come and find out!

This puppet show is specially designed for children ages three through eight and their parents. Telling stories is an important reading development skill. Have fun hearing stories that you'll want to read again and again.

Date (and day of week): _____

At (library name & address, room number or area)

_____

MRS. KNOW-IT-ALL GAME SHOW: WHO SAYS THAT?

Related Themes: Animal sounds, Animals, Colors, Listening

Overview: Children love to mimic animal sounds. It is no wonder that a large number of picture books encourage interaction with animal sounds. This puppet show is about listening to clues, making animal sounds, and saying the name of the animal. Audience participation is encouraged.

The puppet show centers around Mrs. Know-It-All guessing animal identities based on clues and sounds. As usual, she cannot get it right. She needs the audience to help her out.

Early Literacy Skill Focus: Mimicking animal sounds reinforces *phonological awareness*. We use sounds from our own language to create words that "copy" those made by animals. The Literacy To Go handout and the suggested display offer titles that will permit parents and children to interact with literature through mimicking animal sounds.

Check out the short picture book called *Animals Speak* by Lila Prap (New York: North-South Books, 2006). This book gives the sounds that animals make in forty-one different languages. It contains a pronunciation guide and really brings home the point that an English translation of animal noises is based on the sounds used in our language. Other languages use their combination of sounds to "translate" animal speech.

Other Literacy Opportunities:

- **Vocabulary:** Acquainting children with the words used to describe animal sounds is also a vocabulary-building exercise.

- **Phonological awareness:** This skill is supported by the Literacy To Go display and take home tips. *Onomatopoeia* refers to a word that imitates the sound it is describing. *Cluck, neigh, bow-wow,* and *meow* are onomatopoeias formed by sounds used in speech. Playing with the sounds of our language by incorporating a fun activity, such as making animal noises, helps to build an awareness of sound. Just like rhyming and singing, making animal noises is a fun way for children to build phonological awareness.

    To prepare for the puppet show, use the additional puppets from the Literacy To Go display to engage the audience in making animal sounds. Put the puppet on your hand and ask the audience what sound this animal makes. Then repeat the sound they made and ask them, "Who says that?" For example, put on a bear puppet. The audience will tell you that it says "GRRR". Then say, "You're right! GRRR. Who says that?" They'll respond "A bear."

Materials Needed:

- Puppets: Piggy Rae (wearing her pink feather boa), Mrs. Know-It-All, Green Snake, Green Frog, Lamb.

- Props: Bandana, scarf, or eyeshades to act as a blindfold for Mrs. Know-It-All.

- Additional puppets to decorate Literacy To Go display table.

- Literacy To Go handouts for participants (see pp. 110–11).

- Promotional flyers (see p. 112).

- Display books for checkout; use titles provided on the Literacy To Go handout.

- Titles for read-alouds.

Preparation:

A few weeks or more before the program

- Decide on your program theme.
- Announce the storytime program in the library Web site and newsletter.
- Reproduce the promotional flyer (p. 112), and distribute copies to caregivers at the library.

A week or two before the program

- Select and gather your read-aloud titles, as well as display books for checkout, puppets, and props.
- Collect additional puppet animals to decorate the Literacy To Go table.
- Reproduce the Literacy To Go materials (see pp. 110–11).
- Practice the read-aloud books and the puppet play.

On the day of the program

- Create a display of checkout material based on the phonological awareness literacy skill of books that feature animal sounds.
- Decorate the Literacy To Go display table with additional puppets that are not in the puppet show.

Puppet Show Performance Tips: A convenient way to take Mrs. Know-It-All off the stage when you change animal contestant puppets is for her to say that she needs to adjust her blindfold, that she needs a drink of water, or something along those lines. This way, you can use two hands to put the next puppet on your other hand.

Play up the sounds the animals make while they are talking with Mrs. Know-It-All. Have the snake extend his "sssss," the frog can interject an occasional "Ribbet," etc.

The Program

During the read-aloud segment: After welcoming the participants, gather the children and caregivers into a semicircle around your storytelling chair. Read aloud books that encourage audience participation with animal sounds. Or read one of your selected read-alouds and then have the audience help you mimic the sounds of the animals that you read about.

Introduce the puppet show: Have the group assemble comfortably around the puppet stage. As leader, address the group with the following welcome.

> I had such fun reading stories to you today. Thank you for helping me by being good listeners and making animal sounds with me. Now I'm going to do a puppet show for you, and I need your help again. Mrs. Know-It-All is going to hear an animal sound and try to guess which animal makes that sound. Sometimes we'll ask you to make that animal sound with us, and sometimes we'll need you to tell Mrs. Know-It-All what kind of animal it is. So put on your thinking caps and your listening ears, and let's get started with our puppet show.

Move to your place behind the puppet stage to begin the show.

After the puppet show: Bring Mrs. Know-It-All out to the front with you after the puppet show. Ask the audience if they want to play "Who Says That?" Use one of the puppets from the Literacy To Go display and ask the audience what that animal says. Be prepared to have Mrs. Know-It-All guess some wrong answers. Allow the audience to tell her the correct animal and then have Mrs. Know-It-All profess, "I knew that! I'm Mrs. Know-It-All, and I know everything!" Kids love to tell Mrs. Know-It-All that she does not know everything.

Tell caregivers that interacting with the literature by mimicking animal sounds and encouraging their children to follow suit helps to bring the written word to life. The titles chosen for the display encourage this kind of interaction and will help the child to develop the early literacy skill of phonological awareness.

Have the puppets tell the children good-bye.

MRS. KNOW-IT-ALL GAME SHOW: WHO SAYS THAT?

Puppets:

Piggy Rae (wearing her pink feather boa)

Mrs. Know-It-All

Green Snake (can use green sock puppet)

Green Frog

White Lamb

Props:

Blindfold (bandanna, scarf, or eyeshades—whatever will stay on the Mrs. Know-It-All Puppet)

[Enter Piggy Rae.]

PIGGY RAE: Hi, y'all!!!! Hi, hi, hi. Yes, it is I, the famous Piggy Rae. Winner of the Miss Pork Rind Beauty Contest in 2001, now a famous way, way, way off Broadway actress. Today I will be the guest co-hostess of the *Mrs. Know-It-All Game Show.* Yeaaaa!!! All you lucky fans will get to see me today as we try to stump Mrs. Know-It-All. Let us waste no further time, as I introduce our hostess, Mrs. Know-It-All!!!! Come on; let me hear a round of applause! It's Mrs. Know-It-All!

MRS. KNOW-IT-ALL: Hello, hello, hello. Buenos dias, as they say in France!

PIGGY RAE: Y'all, Buenos dias is "good morning" in Spanish, not French.

MRS. KNOW-IT-ALL: Buenos dias is Spanish?

PIGGY RAE: Of course.

MRS. KNOW-IT-ALL: Buenos dias is "good morning" in Spanish. Hmmm, . . . I knew that, because I am Mrs. Know-It-All, and I know everything!

PIGGY RAE:	Y'all . . . I don't think she knew that. But, can all of y'all please say "Buenos dias" to Mrs. Know-It-All? Boys and girls, let's say good morning in Spanish. Repeat after me.
	"Buenos dias."
	[Audience repeats:] "Buenos dias."
	Very good! Muy bien! Now let's get started with our show. We are going to have fun today.
MRS. KNOW-IT-ALL:	Indeed we shall. Today's show is called "Who Says That?" I, Mrs. Know-It-All, will gather clues about animal contestants, until I can very skillfully and cleverly detect the identity of the animal.
PIGGY RAE:	For example, if I give her the clue "I am a pet and I say "Meow," Mrs. Know-It-All will say . . . .
MRS. KNOW-IT-ALL:	You are a pet and you say "Meow." Hmmm, . . . You are a dog.
PIGGY RAE:	No, it is not a dog. Dogs do not say "Meow."
MRS. KNOW-IT-ALL:	I knew that!
PIGGY RAE:	Really? What do dogs say?
MRS. KNOW-IT-ALL:	Not "Meow."
PIGGY RAE:	No.
MRS. KNOW-IT-ALL:	"Chirp, chirp"?
PIGGY RAE:	No. Not "chirp, chirp." I think we should ask the boys and girls in our audience, they'll know what dogs say.
MRS. KNOW-IT-ALL:	Hmm, . . . Yes, perhaps we should ask our studio audience. Boys and girls, what do dogs say?
	[Allow time for audience to respond.]
MRS. KNOW-IT-ALL:	Of course. Dogs say, "Woof, woof." I knew that because I am Mrs. Know-It-All , and I know everything!
PIGGY RAE:	And our original clue, which was, "I am a pet and I say 'Meow.' Boys and girls, I ask you, "Who says that?"
	[Allow time for audience to respond.]

Exactly correct. Cats say, "Meow." Boys and girls, please meow like a cat for Mrs. Know-It-All.

[Allow time for audience to respond.]

Very nice! And that is how we play our game show, "Who Says That?"

MRS. KNOW-IT-ALL: STOP! I know the answer. It is a cat. A cat is a pet and it says "Meow." Also, dogs are pets and they say, "Woof, woof!" I'm Mrs. Know-It-All, and I know everything.

PIGGY RAE: The boys and girls in our studio audience just said that. Cats say "Meow." Isn't that what you boys and girls just said?

[Allow time for audience to respond.]

MRS. KNOW-IT-ALL: Well, in that case, I think we need to thank our audience for their help with this one. Boys and girls, give yourselves a round of applause.

[Allow time for audience to respond.]

PIGGY RAE: Yeaaaa! Good for y'all! Now that you know how the game is played, let's begin. We will put a blindfold on Mrs. Know-It-All so she cannot peek. Our guest animals will help with the clues. Okay y'all, don't go away; we'll be right back.

[Take puppets offstage and put a blindfold on Mrs. Know-It-All.]

[Mrs. Know-It-All, blindfolded, and Piggy Rae reenter.]

MRS. KNOW-IT-ALL: Helloooo? Is anyone there? I cannot see a thing. Boys and girls? Helloooo?

PIGGY RAE: Don't worry, Mrs. Know-It-All, your studio audience is still here. Boys and girls, tell Mrs. Know-It-All, "Let's play 'Who Says That?'" Okay? Repeat after me:

"Let's play 'Who Says That?'"

[Audience repeats:] "Let's play 'Who Says That?'"

MRS. KNOW-IT-ALL: Oh, I'm so glad that you all stayed, but I knew you would, because I am Mrs. Know-It-All, and I know everything. I'm glad to know you are there.

PIGGY RAE:	Mrs. Know-It-All, are you ready for your first clue? Is that blindfold in place?
MRS. KNOW-IT-ALL:	Absolutely! And I am ready for my first clue.
PIGGY RAE:	Okay then. I will wait offstage and send out our first contestant. [She exits.] [Offstage.] Here is your first animal contestant with your first clue. [Enter snake puppet.]
SNAKE:	I am the color green, and I am long and sssssssssskinny.
MRS. KNOW-IT-ALL:	You are long and skinny and green—you are a stick. A stick is the color green and is long and skinny.
SNAKE:	No, I'm not a ssssssssstick. I am an animal who is long and sssssskinny and green.
MRS. KNOW-IT-ALL:	I knew that.
SNAKE:	Here is your next clue. I can wrap mysssself around thingssssss.
MRS. KNOW-IT-ALL:	Are you a vine? A green, creepy, crawly vine?
SNAKE:	No.
MRS. KNOW-IT-ALL:	Are you wrapping paper?
SNAKE:	NO! Let me give you one more clue: I say HISSSSSSSSSSSSSS. Mrs. Know-It-All, I ask you: who says that?
MRS. KNOW-IT-ALL:	That is too easy! You say HISSSSSSSSSSSSSSSS. You are a leaky balloon! Leaky balloons say HISSSSSSSSSSSSSSS.
SNAKE:	No, I am not a leaky balloon. Boys and girls, can you say hissssss like I do? Let's all hissss for Mrs. Know-It-All. [Allow time for audience to respond.] That was an excellent hisssss . . . .
MRS. KNOW-IT-ALL:	Stop! I know who you are. You are a leaky tire. They hissssss . . . .

SNAKE:	No, I am an animal that is green and long and skinny, I wrap myself around things, and I say HISSSSSSSSSSSSS. Boys and girls, can you tell Mrs. Know-It-All who I am?
	[Allow time for audience to say "snake."]
MRS. KNOW-IT-ALL:	Of course! You are a snake. I knew that because am Mrs. Know-It-All , and I know everything! Bravo, Snake. Thank you for being a contestant on the *Mrs. Know-It-All Game Show.*
	[Snake exits.]
PIGGY RAE:	[Reenters.] I think that we should thank the boys and girls for helping us guess, "Who Says That?"
MRS. KNOW-IT-ALL:	Perhaps they helped a little. Now for my next contestant. I hope this one will be a little bit more difficult. That snake was very easy for me to guess.
PIGGY RAE:	All right. Let's bring on the next contestant and play, "Who Says That?"
MRS. KNOW-IT-ALL:	Ready when you are.
	[Piggy Rae exits.]
PIGGY RAE:	[Offstage.] Is that blindfold still in place?
MRS. KNOW-IT-ALL:	Yes, it is.
	[Enter frog puppet.]
FROG:	Ribbet! I am the color green.
MRS. KNOW-IT-ALL:	Stop! You are a snake! A green, slithery snake who says, "Hissss."
FROG:	No, I am not a snake!
MRS. KNOW-IT-ALL:	But you just said you were green. My last contestant was green, and he was a snake!
FROG:	But Mrs. Know-It-All, more than one animal is green. Ribbet! Turtles are green.
MRS. KNOW-IT-ALL:	You are a turtle! I'm Mrs. Know-It-All, and I know everything. You are a green turtle.

FROG: That was just an example. I'm not a turtle. Let me finish my clues. I say, "ribbet, ribbet." Boys and girls, can you help me? Tell Mrs. Know-It-All what sound I make. Say it after me, please. "Ribbet, ribbet."

[audience repeats:] "Ribbet, ribbet."

Thank you, boys and girls. Now Mrs. Know-It-All, I ask you, "Who says that?"

MRS. KNOW-IT-ALL: A sewing machine? A car?

FROG: No, I am an animal. Boys and girls, please help me. I'm green, I hop, and I say "ribbet, ribbet." Tell Mrs. Know-It-All, "Who says that?"

[Allow time for audience to say "frog."]

MRS. KNOW-IT-ALL: A frog? Why of course, I should have known. A green, hoppy, ribbeting frog! That was my next guess. Now I'm getting all warmed up, bring me one more animal contestant. I'll get the next one right on my first try, because I am Mrs. Know-It-All, and I know everything.

FROG: Yes, I am a frog. Thank you, boys and girls, for helping Mrs. Know-It-All. Here comes the next contestant.

[Exit frog.]

MRS. KNOW-IT-ALL: I'm certainly lucky that I have such a clever studio audience here with me today.

[Enter lamb.]

LAMB: Baa. Here I am, Mrs. Know-It-All, with your first clue. I am white and fluffy.

MRS. KNOW-IT-ALL: You are a fluffy, white cloud. Clouds are white and very fluffy.

LAMB: No, I am an aaaanimal.

MRS. KNOW-IT-ALL: I knew that.

LAMB: The next clue is:

My wool keeps people warm in the winter.

MRS. KNOW-IT-ALL: Warm in winter? You are a furnace.

LAMB: That is not correct. I am not a furnace.

MRS. KNOW-IT-ALL:	A polar bear? Polar bears must be warm in winter. And a polar bear is white.
LAMB:	That was a good guess, but polar bears do not have wool. Here is your last clue. I say BAAAAAAAAAAA. I ask you, Mrs. Know-It-All, who says thaaaaaat?
MRS. KNOW-IT-ALL:	I know exactly what you are. You are a baby. Only a baby would say BAAAAAAAAAAA, BAAAAAAAA, WHAAAAAAAA. [Cries like a baby.] WHAAAAAAAA!!!!
LAMB:	Boys and girls, I do not say BAAAAAAAAA, BAAAAAAAAA, WHAAAAAAAA. [Cries like a baby.] Please tell Mrs. Know-It-All what sound I make.
	[Allow time for audience to say "Baa."]
MRS. KNOW-IT-ALL:	You say baaaa . . . .
LAMB:	Yes, but I am not a baby. Boys and girls, let's help Mrs. Know-It-All. I am a white, fluffy animal who says BAAAAAAAAAAAA. Tell Mrs. Know-It-All, who says that?
	[Allow time for audience to say "lamb."]
MRS. KNOW-IT-ALL:	I've got it! You are a lamb. I knew that, because I am Mrs. Know-It-All, and I know everything.
LAMB:	Thank you boys and girls! You were right. My woolly fur helps keep people warm, I am a white and fluffy. I say BAAAAAAAAAAAAA. I am a laaaaaaaaaaaamb. BAAAAAAAAAAAA. [Lamb exits.]
MRS KNOW-IT-ALL:	You see, it is impossible to fool Mrs. Know-It-All!
PIGGY RAE:	[Reenters.] Y'all! I'm beginning to think that there are a few things that Mrs. Know-It-All does not know. We have one more animal as a special guest on today's show. Mrs. Know-It-All, is your blindfold still in place?
MRS. KNOW-IT-ALL:	Yes, it is. I cannot see a thing. I'm ready for the final contestant on "Who Says That?"
PIGGY RAE:	Here is your first clue. I won the Miss Pork Rind Beauty Contest in 2001, I am a famous way, way, way off Broadway actress. And, I am gorgeous.

MRS. KNOW-IT-ALL: Are you a peacock? A peacock is gorgeous.

PIGGY RAE: Good guess, but no. I am pink and I wear a pink feather boa. Pink is my favorite color. Did I mention that I am gorgeous?

MRS. KNOW-IT-ALL: Pink? Are you a flamingo?

PIGGY RAE: No, I am not a flamingo.

MRS. KNOW-IT-ALL: A valentine? A valentine is pink. My guess is a valentine!

PIGGY RAE: I am not a valentine. And here is your final clue: occasionally, and only after I have eaten too much pizza, I may be heard to say [Snort, snort]. I ask you, Mrs. Know-It-All, who says that?

MRS. KNOW-IT-ALL: Snort, snort? That is a very curious sound. Snort, snort. That's the sound my grandpa makes when he is sleeping. Are you my grandpa?

PIGGY RAE: Oh for heaven's sake, take off that ridiculous blindfold!

[She pulls the blindfold off Mrs. Know-It-All.]

MRS. KNOW-IT-ALL: Oh! All I see is you, Piggy Rae.

PIGGY RAE: Finally, you get one right. It is I! The gorgeous, famous actress, beauty queen, very pink Piggy Rae!

MRS. KNOW-IT-ALL: Oh, I get it! Pink, gorgeous, Of course it is you, Piggy Rae. Famous way, way, way off Broadway actress and co-hostess of the *Mrs. Know-It All Game Show.* Yeaaaa! And of course I got it right. That is why they call me Mrs. Know-It-All, because I know everything.

PIGGY RAE: And don't forget our clever studio audience, who helped us out on today's show. Give yourselves a round of applause! Yeaaaa!

MRS. KNOW-IT-ALL: And let's give a big round of applause for our animal contestants: green snake, green frog, white lamb, and the very pink Piggy Rae.

[All exit.]

The End

LITERACY TO GO

Dear Parents and Caregivers,

Some of the very first sounds that children enjoy mimicking are animal sounds, and it is always fun for parents and children to make these sounds together as the child grows up. The booklist offered below contains titles that will permit interaction among you, your child, and the literature.

Playing with the sounds that make up our language prepares children to sound out words when they are ready to become readers. This important prereading skill is called phonological awareness.

Enjoy sharing these books with your children. They'll make you growl, bark, cluck, and moo.

See you next week!

Literacy To Go Take Home Menu

Books that build phonological awareness by using animal sounds: These books invite participation and interaction through mimicking animal sounds. Encourage your child to repeat the sounds after you as you read these books together.

Baddiel, Ivor, and Sophie Jubb. *Cock-a-Doodle Quack! Quack!*
> Baby rooster learns how to say cock-a-doodle-doo!

Beil, Karen Magnuson. *Mooove Over!: A Book About Counting by Twos.*
> A noisy cow wants more space to herself, so she tells the other animals to "mooove over!"

Butler, John. *Can You Growl Like a Bear?*
> Each page invites the readers to make an animal sound.

Cronin, Doreen. *Dooby Dooby Moo.*
> With much revelry, farm animals compete in a talent show.

Dallas-Conté, Julie. *Cock-a-moo-moo.*
> A rooster get help from the barnyard animals to remember how to cock-a-doodle-doo.

Davis, Katie. *Who Hoots?*
> Who hoots, who buzzes, who squeaks . . . ?

DiPucchio, Kelly S. *What's the Magic Word?*
> A cow thinks the magic word is "moo"; a pig says it's "oink." What is the magic word?

Fleming, Denise. *The Cow Who Clucked.*
> The cow looks everywhere for her lost "moo."

Godwin, Laura. *What the Baby Hears.*
> Baby bear hears grr, grr, grr; kitten hears purr, purr, purr.

Kuskin, Karla. *Roar and More.*
> This book will make you roar, hiss, and more.

Kutner, Merrily. *Down on the Farm.*
> A noisy, active, farmyard adventure.

Lawrence, John. *This Little Chick.*
> An entertaining little chick learns to talk to the animals in their own language.

MacDonald, Margaret Read. *A Hen, a Chick, and a String Guitar.*
> A musical story with animal sounds.

Martin, Bill, Jr. *Polar Bear, Polar Bear, What Do You Hear?*

A popular and much-loved animal sound story.

McGee, Marni. *The Noisy Farm: Lots of Animal Noises to Enjoy!*

And lots of animal sounds to mimic!

Most, Bernard. *The Cow That Went Oink.*

A classic moo and oink story.

Murphy, Yannick. *Ahwooooooooo!*

Help teach a wolf to howl at the moon.

Palatini, Margie. *Moo, Who?*

After an accident with a flying cow pie, a cow forgets what she is supposed to say.

Parenteau, Shirley. *One Frog Sang.*

A counting story with many ways to mimic frog sounds.

Pedersen, Janet. *Millie Wants to Play.*

A baby calf and her friends wake up before the rooster crows.

Polacco, Patricia. *Mommies Say Shhh!*

An active farmyard, but mommy holds baby quietly, saying, "Shhh."

Taylor, Thomas. *The Loudest Roar.*

A small tiger startles his jungle friends with his roar.

Walton, Rick. *Herd of Cows! Flock of Sheep! Quiet! I'm Tired! I Need My Sleep!*

The farmer is so sleepy that even the most raucous of animals can't seem to wake him up.

Whybrow, Ian. *The Noisy Way to Bed.*

Just before the reader says the word *bed*, a noisy animal interrupts.

You're Invited to a
PUPPET SHOW!
Come to storytime and a special puppet show performance of

THE MRS. KNOW-IT-ALL GAME SHOW: WHO SAYS THAT?

Who says "meow"? Mrs. Know-It-All is at it again! She tries her best to guess which animals are making sounds. But she needs your help. Please come to our puppet play and teach Mrs. Know-It-All a few things that she doesn't know.

Our puppet show is specially designed for children ages three through eight and their parents, and will help build phonological awareness through animal sounds.

Date (and day of week): _____

At (library name & address, room number or area)

_____

MRS. KNOW-IT-ALL GAME SHOW: MIND YOUR MANNERS

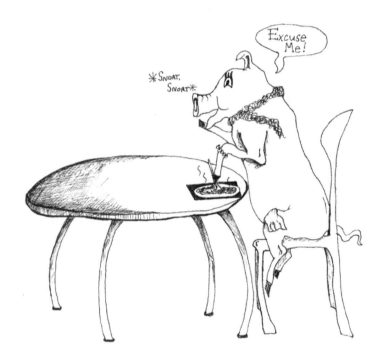

Related Theme: Manners, Self-expression

Overview: An important aspect of vocabulary development is learning and using common, everyday language. The early literacy lesson in this storytime emphasizes being polite and using polite words.

In the puppet play, Piggy Rae and the audience help Mrs. Know-It-All mind her manners.

Early Literacy Skill Focus: The early literacy focus for this puppet show is *vocabulary*, specifically polite words and phrases like "please," "thank you," and "excuse me." The books listed for the Literacy To Go display emphasize adjectives, adverbs, and other useful everyday words. After Mrs. Know-It-All uses impolite phrases, Piggy Rae will prompt the audience to help her use her best manners.

Before or after the puppet skit, you may wish to sing some songs from the book *Are You Quite Polite? Silly Dilly Manners Songs,* by Alan Katz (New York: Margaret K. McElderry Books, 2006). One of the songs in the book is about library manners, sung to the tune of "Twinkle, Twinkle, Little Star." Singing also reinforces the *phonological awareness* skill. Write the words on an easel or wipe-off board and have Piggy Rae lead the audience in singing it.

Other Literacy Opportunities:

- **Vocabulary:** Vocabulary building through the use of everyday words and phrases is supported by the Literacy To Go display and take home tips. Before the puppet show, talk to parents about reinforcing vocabulary development with their children by emphasizing the importance of talking in complete sentences and helping children to speak in complete sentences. Vocabulary words used in the puppet show are:

    - *Rude*: not courteous
    - *Impolite*: exhibiting bad manners
    - *Parched*: very thirsty
    - *Excuse me*: pardon me; sorry
    - May I please?: a courteous request that is more polite than "can I?"

- **Print awareness:** Reinforce print awareness by drawing attention to the words of the song written on the easel or wipe-off board. Tell the children that you wrote the words of the song on the board so that their parents can read it and join in singing it together.

- **Letter knowledge:** Choose a letter from the display or wipe-off board to highlight, for example, the *L* in library. Have the audience hold up their left hands and make an *L* with their index fingers and thumbs extended. That *L* can them distinguish between their left and their right.

Materials Needed:

- Puppets: Piggy Rae (wearing her pink feather boa), Mrs. Know-It-All.
- No special props are needed for this puppet show.
- Easel or wipe-off board (if singing a song from the Alan Katz book mentioned above).
- Literacy To Go handouts for participants (see pp. 122–23).
- Promotional flyers (see p. 124).
- Display books for checkout; use the titles provided on the Literacy To Go handout.
- Titles for read-alouds.

Preparation:

A few weeks or more before the program

- Decide on your program theme.
- Announce the storytime program in the library Web site and newsletter.
- Reproduce the promotional flyer (p. 124), and distribute copies to caregivers at the library.

A week or two before the program

- Select and gather your read-aloud titles, as well as display books for checkout and puppets.
- Reproduce the Literacy To Go materials (see pp. 122–23).
- On the easel of wipe-off board, write the words to the song from the Alan Katz book mentioned above.
- Practice the read-aloud books and the puppet play.

On the day of the program

- Create a display of checkout material based on the vocabulary theme of useful words and phrases.

- Put up the easel or wipe-off board with the song words on it.

Puppet Show Performance Tips: When the audience laughs at the rude responses from Mrs. Know-It-All, be prepared to stop talking until the laughter subsides. Sometimes it is difficult to hear the crowd when you are behind the puppet stage, so listen carefully and try not to talk over them.

The Program

During the read-aloud segment: After welcoming the participants, gather the children and caregivers into a semicircle around your storytelling chair. Read your selected literature.

Before singing any songs, point out to the caregivers that you have written the words on the easel display or wipe-off board, so they can join in singing with you. Tell the children that you have written the words to the songs. Point out a few letters, for example the *L* in library.

Just before you begin the puppet show, sing together the song from *Are You Quite Polite?* (see above). Use Piggy Rae to lead the audience.

Introduce the puppet show: Have the group assemble comfortably around the puppet stage. As leader, address the group with the following welcome.

> In today's puppet show, Mrs. Know-It-All needs a reminder to be polite. Piggy Rae will give her some good advice, but we'll need you to help her remember to say "excuse me," "please," and some other important words. Let's see what happens when Piggy Rae puts manners to the test, in our puppet show called "Mind Your Manners."

Move to your place behind the puppet stage to begin the show.

After the puppet show: Comment about how silly Mrs. Know-It-All is to think that she was using good manners.

Tell caregivers that the books on display all teach vocabulary words, like "please" and "thank you," as well as many other common words and expressions. The selected titles also use descriptive words that are important for children to know in everyday conversation. Encourage them to check out some of the titles.

Have the puppets tell the children good-bye.

You may wish to sing the Alan Katz song again.

MRS. KNOW-IT-ALL GAME SHOW: MIND YOUR MANNERS

Puppets:

> Piggy Rae (wearing her pink feather boa)
>
> Mrs. Know-It-All

[Enter Piggy Rae.]

PIGGY RAE: Hi, y'all!! Welcome to the *Mrs. Know-It-All Game Show*! I'm Piggy Rae, former beauty queen and now a famous way, way, way off Broadway actress. Today I will be the co-hostess of the *Mrs. Know-It-All Game Show*. That's right, all you lucky people will get to see me on today's show!!! Yaaay! Our topic today will be "Mind Your Manners." We will ask Mrs. Know-It-All about the proper and kind way to behave using the best manners.

And now I introduce Mrs. Know-It-All!!!!!!

[Enter Mrs. Know-It-All.]

MRS. KNOW-IT-ALL: Hello! Hello to everyone. I am Mrs. Know-It-All, and I know everything. I know that grass is blue and the sky is green. I know that you put ketchup on cereal and milk on french fries. I know everything because I am Mrs. Know-It-All.

PIGGY RAE: Y'all, I think Mrs. Know-It-All is confused. The sky is not green, it is blue. Grass is green.

MRS. KNOW-IT-ALL: Oh? Blue sky? Green grass? Hmmm. I knew that!

PIGGY RAE: That's not all. You put milk on cereal and ketchup on french fries.

MRS. KNOW-IT-ALL:	That explains a lot. My french fries had been rather soggy with milk. So it's ketchup on french fries. I knew that! Because I am Mrs. Know-It-All, and I know everything.
PIGGY RAE:	That's enough chatter! I'm ready to start the *Mrs. Know-It-All Game Show*. Today's show will teach us excellent manners. Mrs. Know-it-All, here is our first question: What do you do if you are walking down the sidewalk and someone is in your way? What should you say?
MRS. KNOW-IT-ALL:	Yes! I know exactly what to say. If someone is in your way, you say, "Get out of my way! I was here first. Shoo, shoo, I'm coming through."
PIGGY RAE:	I'm sorry, but that would be rude.
MRS. KNOW-IT-ALL:	Rude? What does that mean? I never heard that word before.
PIGGY RAE:	Rude. You know, *rude* means impolite or not nice. You would not tell someone to shoo. That is rude. You say, "Excuse me, may I please pass?" You do not say, "Get out of my way." That is impolite.
MRS. KNOW-IT-ALL:	If someone is in your way, you say, "Excuse me, may I please pass?" You don't say, "Get out of my way?"
PIGGY RAE:	No.
MRS. KNOW-IT-ALL:	You don't say "Shoo?"
PIGGY RAE:	No. Boys and girls, will you help me? Let's all help Mrs. Know-It-All remember to mind her manners. Repeat after me. "Excuse me." [Audience repeats:] "Excuse me!" "May I please pass?" [Audience repeats:] "May I please pass?" Very nice! Thank you.
MRS. KNOW-IT-ALL:	Hmmm, . . . Don't say "Shoo!" Say, "Excuse me, may I please pass?" I knew that!
PIGGY RAE:	Let's continue with our next question on today's show, "Mind Your Manners." Let's pretend that you are at the table and you

accidentally make a rude noise like [Snort, snort]. What would good manners require that you say?

MRS. KNOW-IT-ALL: What if I accidentally said [Snort, snort]? Hmmm, ... [Snort, snort]? Oh I know, I'd say, "[Snort, snort!] Ha, ha, ha, ha! What a funny noise!"

PIGGY RAE: It is not a funny noise! Especially at the table.

MRS. KNOW-IT-ALL: I thought it sounded funny.

PIGGY RAE: No, it is quite rude.

MRS. KNOW-IT-ALL: Another rudeness? Tell me what rude means again.

PIGGY RAE: Boys and girls, please tell Mrs. Know-It-All that rude means impolite.

[Audience says:] "Impolite."

MRS. KNOW-IT-ALL: Would you say "[Snort, snort]. Oops! That was rude, but do you want me to do it again? Ha, ha, ha, ha!"

PIGGY RAE: Absolutely not! You would say "Excuse me."

MRS. KNOW-IT-ALL: You would say, "Excuse me?" I thought you said that when someone is in your way. You mean you say "Excuse me" if you make a rude noise, too? Boys and girls, let's all say "Excuse me" one more time. Apparently it is a very useful and polite phrase. Repeat after me, "Excuse me."

[Audience repeats:] "Excuse me."

Bravo!

PIGGY RAE: Yes. "Excuse me" is a good phrase to know. I say it several times a day. [Snort, snort] Excuse me! See what I mean?

MRS. KNOW-IT-ALL: I noticed that!

PIGGY RAE: Okay, here is the next test of polite behavior on our show, "Mind Your Manners." If you are really thirsty and you need a glass of water, what do you say?

MRS. KNOW-IT-ALL: "Somebody hurry up and get me something to drink. I'm thirsty! Hurry! People are drying up here!"

PIGGY RAE:	That would be rude, rude, rude, and at my house, if I said that I would never get a drink.
MRS. KNOW-IT-ALL:	Maybe you should say, "Get a move on, I'm parched!"
PIGGY RAE:	Rude!
MRS. KNOW-IT-ALL:	Do you say "Excuse me?" You said that was a useful phrase.
PIGGY RAE:	Well, you could say, "Excuse me," but then you would say, "May I please have a glass of cool, refreshing water?"
MRS. KNOW-IT-ALL:	Oh! You say, "May I please." I knew that! Because I am Mrs. Know-it-All, and I know everything.
PIGGY RAE:	You can say "May I please" for many things. Let's practice. Boys and girls, repeat after me. "May I please go outside and play?" [Audience repeats:] "May I please go outside and play?" Good job! How about this one: "May I please have a cookie?" [Audience repeats:] "May I please have a cookie?" Perfect! Let's do another! "May I please play quietly and then go have a nap?" [Audience repeats:] "May I please play quietly and then go have a nap?" Ha! Ha! Ha! I bet that's the first time you ever asked for that!
MRS. KNOW-IT-ALL:	Ha! Ha! Ha! Piggy Rae! You are very funny! I have a Little Miss Know-It-All at home, and she has never said, "May I please play quietly and then go have a nap?" I would like to hear that again. Boys and girls, let's say that one more time. Repeat after me, "May I please play quietly and then go have a nap?" [Audience repeats:] "May I please play quietly and then go have a nap?" Lovely!
PIGGY RAE:	But back to reality. We were talking about minding our manners and asking politely for a glass of water. Mrs. Know-It-All, what would you say after you get the glass of water?

MRS. KNOW-IT-ALL:	Hmmm, . . . Do you say, "Get me another. I said I was drying up!"
PIGGY RAE:	No.
MRS. KNOW-IT-ALL:	Do you say, "Excuse me, get me another. I said I was drying up!"
PIGGY RAE:	No.
MRS. KNOW-IT-ALL:	Do you say [Pretending to cry,], "I didn't want it in that ugly glass. I wanted it in my mermaid glass!!! WHAAAA . . ."?
PIGGY RAE:	Heavens, NO!
MRS. KNOW-IT-ALL:	Do you say [Pretending to cry.], "Excuse me; I didn't want it in that glass. . . . WHAAAA!"?
PIGGY RAE:	NO!
MRS. KNOW-IT-ALL:	Stop! I know what you say! You say, "More, more, more, more!"
PIGGY RAE:	Absolutely not! You say, "Thank you!"
MRS. KNOW-IT-ALL:	"Thank you?" I knew that!
PIGGY RAE:	Boys and girls, we need your help again. Repeat after me, "Thank you."
	[Audience repeats:] "Thank you."
	No, thank YOU! [Pause.] I insist, thank YOU! [Pause.] Okay, just being silly again. You know me. Piggy Rae, famous way, way, way off Broadway actress!
MRS. KNOW-IT-ALL:	Well, I will be serious, and say that now I know excellent manners! I can say, "Excuse me," "May I please," and "Thank you!" I'm Mrs. Know-it-All, and I know everything about minding my manners! And now I have a question for you, Piggy Rae!
PIGGY RAE:	A question for me? Finally, someone will actually get something right around here. I'm ready, ask away!

MRS. KNOW-IT-ALL:	What do you say if someone tells you that you look gorgeous in a pink feather boa?
PIGGY RAE:	Why that's easy. You say, "Of course I do! I look gorgeous in pink. I'm beautiful and talented. I am Piggy Rae. Miss Pork Rind 2001. Of course I look gorgeous in pink, it's my favorite color!"
MRS. KNOW-IT-ALL:	Oh, my dear! That is most improper! All you do is say two simple words. You just say, "Thank you!"
PIGGY RAE:	Thank you?
MRS. KNOW-IT-ALL:	Thank you.
PIGGY RAE:	Thank you. When someone says something nice about you, you just say, "Thank you." Oh. How pleasant. Just say, "Thank you." That sounds like something that a famous, gorgeous pig, such as I, would say. It's so me! I love it! THANK YOU! THANK YOU!
MRS. KNOW-IT-ALL:	Let's practice that with the boys and girls in our audience. Piggy Rae, you tell them something nice and then they can say, "Thank you."
PIGGY RAE:	Oh yes, of course I will. Boys and girls, you have wonderful manners.
	[Audience should now say:] "Thank you." [Prompt if necessary.]
	You're welcome. And it was a pleasure to have you in our studio audience on the *Mrs. Know-It-All Game Show*, "Mind Your Manners."
	[Audience should now say:] "Thank you." [Prompt if necessary.]
	You're welcome. I'm Piggy Rae . . . .
MRS. KNOW-IT-ALL:	And I'm Mrs. Know-it-All, reminding you to use your best manners.
PIGGY RAE:	Bye-bye now.
	[Both puppets exit.]

The End

LITERACY TO GO

Dear Parents and Caregivers,

We enjoyed having you and your children attend our storytime today. Today's Literacy To Go tips and book suggestions involve vocabulary, specifically useful everyday words and phrases.

The puppet show, "The Mrs. Know-It-All Game Show: Mind Your Manners," used humor to encourage us to be polite. Piggy Rae taught Mrs. Know-It-All to use her best manners, and Piggy Rae, gorgeous in her pink feather boa, needed a small lesson in humility.

The suggested titles in our Literacy To Go list include common words and phrases that will help your child build a useful vocabulary. Knowing the names of things and knowing how to describe things are important prereading skills.

See you next week.

Literacy To Go Take Home Menu

Books that build vocabulary—useful descriptive words and phrases: You can reinforce language development by using some of these descriptive words when talking to your child.

Beaumont, Karen. *I Ain't Gonna Paint No More.*
An engaging read-aloud with a surprise ending. Focuses on color words, body parts, and rhyme.

Dewdney, Anna. *Llama, Llama Mad at Mama.*
Descriptive adjectives are used to describe this shopping adventure. Includes a lesson on using proper manners.

Dunbar, Joyce. *Shoe Baby.*
Shoe baby goes places with a very kind "How do you do?"

Gliori, Debi. *Flora's Blanket.*
Name all the places that Flora's family hunts for her missing blanket.

Hindley, Judy. *Baby Talk: A Book of First Words and Phrases.*
Introduces important words from a baby's day at the playground, at mealtime, and at bedtime.

Jenkins, Steve. *Move!*
Animals move by leaping, running, and crawling.

Katz, Alan. *Are You Quite Polite? Silly Dilly Manners Songs.*
Kids will laugh out loud at the funny songs that teach good manners through bad examples.

Levin, Bridget. *Rules of the Wild: An Unruly Book of Manners.*
What is the definition of good manners? Animals and people have different rules.

Rosenthal, Amy Krouse. *Cookies: Bite-size Life Lessons.*
A wonderful way to learn new vocabulary words—taught with cookies.

Sierra, Judy. *Mind Your Manners, B. B. Wolf.*
The Big Bad Wolf behaves himself in the retirement village.

Spinelli, Eileen. *When You Are Happy.*
Build vocabulary by talking about feelings and sensations. Your family takes care of you when you are cold, grumpy, sick, etc.

Weatherford, Carole Boston. *Jazz Baby.*
This rhythmical book introduces names of musical instruments.

Wells, Rosemary. *Yoko's World of Kindness: Golden Rules for a Happy Classroom.*
Getting along with others, teasing, and separation anxiety are presented in six short stories, along with reinforcing vocabulary development.

You're Invited to a
PUPPET SHOW!
Come to storytime and a special puppet show performance of

THE MRS. KNOW-IT-ALL GAME SHOW: MIND YOUR MANNERS

Mrs. Know-It-All proves again that she does not know everything. She needs you to help her learn better manners. Won't you please come and help her out?

Our puppet show is specially designed for children ages three through eight and their parents, and will help build vocabulary.

Date (and day of week): _____

At (library name & address, room number or area)

_____

We hope to see you!

MY FAVORITE COLORS (MIS COLORES FAVORITOS)

Related Themes: Colors, Spanish, Concepts, Languages

Overview: The concept of colors in both English and Spanish is the focus of this storytime. Children name colors in both languages and play guessing games with the puppets.

In the puppet play, Señorita Lana, the Spanish teacher, asks the puppets to talk about their favorite color. Each puppet gives clues about a color in the form of a rhyme or riddle, and the audience tries to guess it. Then Señorita Lana says the color in Spanish and the audience repeats it.

Early Literacy Skill Focus: *Vocabulary*, specifically the names of the colors in both English and Spanish, are the focus of the literacy activity for this storytime. Children repeat the color names in English and Spanish. The rhyming verses that some animals recite reinforce *phonological awareness. Letter knowledge* of *P* is the focus of Piggy Rae's favorite color (pink).

The Literacy To Go sheet offers caregivers more tips on talking about colors at home.

Other Early Literacy Opportunities:

- **Vocabulary:** Vocabulary development, specifically naming and recognizing colors in both English and Spanish, is the skill supported by the Literacy To go display and take home tips. The puppet show features poems or riddles about colors. It encourages the audience to participate as they try to guess the name of the color in English and repeat the color name in Spanish.

  Each puppet also has an object that is its favorite color. By integrating the visual and the auditory, you help children to retain new vocabulary.

  During the read-aloud segment of your storytime, say the Spanish color words as you point to colors in the books to help introduce the words to the children.

- **Phonological awareness:** Several of the puppets use rhyming words as clues for the audience to guess their favorite color. You may talk about other words that rhyme with colors (such as "Shoe rhymes with blue," or "Bean rhymes with green.")

  Mrs. Know-It-All recites a haiku, which does not rhyme, but requires a specific number of syllables in each line of text. Haiku has three lines, with five syllables in the first and last lines and seven syllables in the middle line. Older children should see the text written on a display easel or wipe-off board, or on a handout, so they can count the syllables per line. You can clap out the syllables with them before or after the puppet show.

- **Letter knowledge:** Piggy Rae shows the letter *P* as she describes her favorite color. Use some pink die-cut letter *P's* as part of the Literacy To Go display.

Materials Needed:

- Puppets: Señorita Lana, Tommy Turtle, Bernie Bear, Alistair McMoose, Piggy Rae (wearing her pink feather boa), Granny, Mrs. Know-It-All.

- Props: green leaf, red paper heart, die cut letter *P* or large letter *P* written in pink on a piece of paper, pink rose (silk flower), rainbow—hand drawn or printed off the Internet.

- Colorful name tags. You may die-cut or hand cut these into any shape you choose. Use a wide range of colors so each child can pick his or her favorite color.

- Crayons and tape so the children can write their names on the name tags and stick them to their shirts.

- Colorful objects (toys, crayons, etc.) for the Literacy To Go display. To reinforce letter knowledge, use colorful die-cut letters of the alphabet as "confetti" on the table. Be sure to include some pink letter *P's*.

- Display easel, wipe-off board, or printed handout with the words to the haiku that Mrs. Know-It-All recites (optional—for older children).

- Literacy To Go handouts for participants (see pp. 140–42).

- Promotional flyers (see p. 143).

- Display books for checkout; use titles provided on the Literacy To Go handout.

- Titles for read-alouds.

Preparation:

A few weeks or more before the program

- Decide on your storytime theme.
- Announce the storytime program in the library Web site and newsletter.
- Reproduce the promotional flyer (p. 143) and distribute copies to caregivers at the library.

A week or two before the program

- Select and gather your read-aloud titles, as well as display books for checkout, puppets, and props.
- Collect colorful objects to decorate the Literacy To Go table—crayons, Legos™, a piñata, toys, bright scarves, etc.
- Write the haiku on the easel or wipe-off board, or type and copy it.
- Reproduce the Literacy To Go materials (see pp. 140–42).
- Die-cut or hand cut name tags.
- Practice the read-aloud books and the puppet play.

On the day of the program

- Create a display of checkout material based on the vocabulary literacy theme of colors.
- Use the colorful objects that you collected to decorate the table.
- Put up the easel or wipe-off board, if using it.
- Provide the colorful name tags, crayons, and tape for the children to use as they enter the storytime space.

Puppet Show Performance Tips: If you have difficulty changing puppets with one hand, add a line for Señorita Lana to excuse herself from the stage. She may say, "Granny, let me help you come to the front of the class," etc.

If you are uncertain how to pronounce the Spanish words, try this Web site, which offers an audible pronunciation guide: www.spanishdict.com/.

When reciting the haiku, remember that the word *orange* has two syllables and *violet* has three syllables.

This puppet show includes all of the stock puppet characters and can be a little bit long for storytime. One option is to conduct a storytime about concepts—shapes, colors, letters, and numbers—and schedule it over a two-week time frame. There is no shortage of wonderful read-alouds for this theme.

Then perform half of this puppet show the first week and the rest of it the second week.

For week one, stop after Alistair McMoose's line, "Well, I guess I better go back and clean up the water in the cloak room. Adios." Señorita Lana replies that all of the students will help him, and she tells the audience that she'll see them next week when she talks to Piggy Rae, Granny, and Mrs. Know-It-All.

For week two, begin with the next line. Señorita Lana says, "Today we have learned the colors green, or verde; red, or rojo; and white, or blanco." Change this line to, "Last week we learned the colors green . . . ." Have the audience repeat the words in both languages.

The Program

During the read-aloud segment: After welcoming participants, gather children and caregivers into a semicircle around your storytelling chair. After reading some of your selected literature, talk about colors using both the English and Spanish words. Point out colors that you see in the room (e.g., the clothing of the boys and girls in the audience). You can also have the puppets participate in the discussion. For example, if you talk about green, have Tommy Turtle do the talking. This will help prepare the children for the puppet show.

Introduce the puppet show: Have the group assemble comfortably around the puppet stage. As leader, address the group with the following welcome.

> Colors help to make our lives exciting. Today you picked your favorite color for your name tag, and now our puppet friends are going to tell us about their favorite colors. The Spanish teacher, Señorita Lana, gives each puppet a turn to give us hints about a color.

> You will help guess that color. So listen carefully to the clues. Then we'll repeat the color name in Spanish. The puppet show is called "My Favorite Colors (Mis Colores Favoritos)."

> Can you all say that with me? "My Favorite Colors."

> [Audience repeats:] "My Favorite Colors."

> "Mis Colores Favoritos" (MEES koh-LOHR-es fa-vo-REE-tos)

> [Audience repeats:] "Mis Colores Favoritos."

> Very good! Muy bien! (moo-ey bee EHN)

> Let's get started now with our show.

Move to your place behind the puppet stage to begin the show.

After the puppet show: Ask the children at the count of three to call out their favorite color. Say, "That's the best color of all!"

Hand out copies of the Literacy To Go sheets to caregivers, explaining that the tips will help the children know color names and look for colors around them. This helps build vocabulary skills. Encourage caregivers to check out the Literacy To Go titles.

Have the puppets tell the children good-bye.

MY FAVORITE COLORS (MIS COLORES FAVORITOS)

Puppets:

Señorita Lana

Tommy Turtle

Bernie Bear

Alistair McMoose

Piggy Rae (wearing her pink feather boa)

Granny

Mrs. Know-It-All

Props:

Leaf

Red paper heart

Die-cut letter *P* (pink) or large letter *P* written in pink on a piece of paper

Pink rose

Rainbow (hand drawn or a color picture from the Internet)

[Enter Señorita Lana.]

SEÑORITA LANA: Hello, boys and girls.

Hola, niños y niñas (OH-lah NEEN-yohs ee NEEN-yahs).

I am Señorita Lana. My name, Señorita, means Miss, and Lana means wool. Can you all say my name? Repeat after me. "Señorita" (sehn-yohr-EET-ah).

[Audience repeats:] "Señorita"

"Lana" (LAH nah).

[Audience repeats:] "Lana."

Very good! Muy bien!

I teach Spanish to your favorite puppets. Today they will each tell us about their favorite color, and then you will learn the Spanish word for it. I cannot wait to hear what they will say. The first student that I call on is Tommy Turtle. Tommy, please come to the head of the class.

[Pause.]

Tommy? Where are you? Dónde estás? (DOHN-deh eh-STAHS)

TOMMY TURTLE: [Offstage.] I'm coming as fast as I can. You know, I'm a turtle and I'm verrrry sloooow.

SEÑORITA LANA: Oh yes, of course. No problem.

TOMMY TURTLE: Here I am. Oh, dear. I wish you hadn't called on me first. I'm very timid.

SEÑORITA LANA: You'll be fine, Tommy. First we want to hear your speech about your favorite color. I will ask the audience, "De qué color es?" (deh KAY koh-LOHR ehs), which means, "What color is this?" We will see if the audience can guess what it is. And then we will all practice saying the Spanish word. Are you ready to begin?

TOMMY TURTLE: Oh dear. [Hides in his shell.] I'm a little shy. I don't like to be in the limelight. That's a hint about my favorite color. LIMElight. But I think I'm ready to start. [Comes out of his shell.]

"My Favorite Color" by Tommy Turtle

This is the color of tasty grass.

A food I like to eat.

And to pass my Spanish class

Would also be a treat.

SEÑORITA LANA: Very good! Muy bien! Tommy Turtle told us that his favorite color is the color of grass. Boys and girls, niños y niñas, de qué color es? Or, what color is this?

[Allow time for audience to say "green."]

Sí. Yes. You are right. It is the color green. The Spanish word for green is verde (VAIR deh). Repeat after me: "Verde."

[Audience repeats:] "Verde."

Very good! Muy bien!

Tommy, thank you for the nice poem. Gracias. Did you bring a sample of the color green for us to see?

TOMMY TURTLE: Yes. Sí. [Tommy exits and returns with a leaf.] I brought myself. I am green! I am verde. And I also brought a green leaf. I like to eat grass and leaves. You could say that I cannot leave them alone!

SEÑORITA LANA: Tommy, you are very funny, especially for someone who thinks he is shy. I think that you will have no problem passing your Spanish class. You get an "A" for today!

TOMMY TURTLE: Oh, my gosh. That makes me very happy! Thank you. Gracias.

SEÑORITA LANA: And hooray for green, verde! Let's all give Tommy a round of applause while he goes back to his seat. Yeaaaa!

[Tommy Turtle exits.]

That was a very good lesson for the color green, verde. Grass is verde, Tommy Turtle is verde, and he brought us a green leaf. Our next student to talk about his favorite color is Bernie Bear. Bernie, will you please come to the front of the class?

BERNIE BEAR: Oh boy! I'm so excited. I wanted to go first, but it's okay to go second. Ohhhh, boy! I'm so excited. I have the best favorite color. You'll see. It's the best and it's my favorite.

SEÑORITA LANA: Well, it sounds like you did your homework, Bernie. Go ahead and tell us about your favorite color.

BERNIE BEAR: "My Riddle About my Favorite Color" by Bernie Bear

In my room I have a BED.

This rhymes with the color _____. [Short Pause.]

Here's another one:

In my garage I have a SLED.

This rhymes with the color _____. [Short pause.]

SEÑORITA LANA: Bernie Bear! Good riddle. Let's see if the boys and girls can help us out here. This color rhymes with bed and sled. Boys and girls, niños y niñas, de qué color es? Or, what color is this? Bed . . . sled . . . _____.

[Allow time for audience to say "red."]

Very good! Muy bien! Sí. Yes. You are right. It is the color red. Let's all say that; repeat after me, Bed . . . sled . . . red.

[Audience repeats:] "Bed . . . sled . . . red.

The Spanish word for red is rojo (ROH hoh). Repeat after me: "Rojo."

[Audience repeats:] "Rojo."

Very good! Muy bien!

Bernie, thank you for that good riddle. Did you bring a sample of your favorite color, red or rojo, to class today?

BERNIE BEAR: Oh yes, it was so hard to choose because red, rojo, is my favorite color and I have a lot of red things. I have my favorite rojo shirt, my favorite rojo tennis shoes, my favorite rojo bicycle, my favorite rojo toothbrush, and my favorite rojo dragon kite. Someday, when I'm big, I'm going to drive a rojo car!

SEÑORITA LANA: So many choices. What did you decide on?

BERNIE BEAR: I decided on this. [He exits and returns with a cutout of a red heart.] A red heart because I love rojo!

SEÑORITA LANA: Very good! Muy bien! How clever of you. Thank you. Gracias. And, hooray for red, rojo! Let's all give Bernie a round of applause while he goes back to his seat. Yeaaaa! So far today all of my students are doing "A+" work. I'm very proud.

BERNIE BEAR: Oh boy! I'm so excited. "A+" work! I might make the honor roll! Wait until my mom and dad hear about this! [He exits.]

SEÑORITA LANA: That was a very good lesson for the color red, rojo. Red rhymes with the words *bed* and *sled*. Bernie made us a red heart because he loves the color rojo. Our next student to talk about his favorite color is Alistair McMoose. Alistair, will you please come to the front of the class?

ALISTAIR McMOOSE: Hola, Señorita Lana.

SEÑORITA LANA: Buenos dias, good morning, Alistair. We have had a very good lesson today, Alistair. Are you ready to talk to us about your favorite color?

ALISTAIR McMOOSE: I chose my favorite color because I live in a very cold climate, mostly Canada and Alaska. Brrrr. The winters are very cold. So here is my clue:

"An Icy Rhyme" by Alistair McMoose

My favorite color

As you might know,

Is fresh and bright

As new fallen snow.

SEÑORITA LANA: There's another excellent clue for a very nice color. Boy and girls, niños y niñas, can you guess what color is as fresh and bright as new fallen snow? De qué color es? Or, what color is this?

[Allow time for audience to say "white."]

Very good! Muy bien! Sí. Yes. It is the color white. The Spanish word for white is blanco (BLAHN koh). Repeat after me: "Blanco."

[Audience repeats:] "Blanco."

And Alistair, did you bring in a sample of the color white, or blanco?

ALISTAIR McMOOSE: I certainly did! I'll be right back. [He exits.]

[Pause.]

SEÑORITA LANA: Alistair? Where are you? Dónde estás?

ALISTAIR McMOOSE: [Offstage.] Just a moment. I cannot find it! I'm looking! I left it right here. [Reenters.] I say, did any of you see my freshly fallen, bright, white snow?

SEÑORITA LANA: Alistair? Did you say that you brought some snow with you?

ALISTAIR McMOOSE: Indeed. I brought a whole handful of snow with me. I put it in my coat pocket so no one would see my clue, and now it is gone! I dare say, we must immediately call the police.

SEÑORITA LANA: Alistair, think about your science lessons. What happens to snow when the temperature rises above freezing?

ALISTAIR McMOOSE: Why it melts, of course . . . . Oh, I see where we are going with this. That explains the rather large puddle of water that is now in the cloak room. I'm sorry. Lo siento. Let's cancel that call to the police department, shall we? Apparently there is no missing snow, only melted snow. Trust me, however, it was the color white, or blanco.

SEÑORITA LANA: Do you have another idea for your sample of something that is white, blanco?

ALISTAIR McMOOSE: I'm rather perplexed. I don't know.

SEÑORITA LANA: Do you see anything at all that is perfectly white?

ALISTAIR McMOOSE: White? Blanco? Where should I look?

SEÑORITA LANA: Look right here.

ALISTAIR McMOOSE: Hmmm, . . .

SEÑORITA LANA: Perhaps we should ask the boys and girls, a los niños y a las niñas. Does anyone see something white?

[Allow time for audience to respond. Wait until someone says Señorita Lana. If no one does, Señorita Lana should ask:] "What about me?"

ALISTAIR McMOOSE: Of course! Señorita Lana! Your coat is white! Your coat is blanco! You are a lamb with a coat of white wool! Of course!

SEÑORITA LANA: Very good! Muy bien! Thank you for your help, boys and girls, niños y niñas. Gracias. I have a white coat. Blanco. Señorita Lana is a white lamb.

ALISTAIR McMOOSE: Well, I guess I better go back and clean up the water in the cloak room. Adios.

SEÑORITA LANA: Today we have learned the colors green, or verde; red, or rojo; and white, or blanco. Our next student to talk about her favorite color is . . . .

PIGGY RAE: Hi, y'all! Hi, hi, hi! It is I, Piggy Rae! Finally! It is my turn. I've been waiting for a very long time for you to call my name. And I'm sure all of my fans have been waiting too.

SEÑORITA LANA: No, Piggy Rae, it is not your turn yet. It is Granny's turn.

PIGGY RAE: Well, Granny is busy. She didn't like the way Alistair was cleaning up the water mess in the closet, and she's making him do it over. Ha, ha, ha. That's Granny for you. She's a tough one. So, I guess it's my turn?

SEÑORITA LANA: Very well, if Granny is busy, you can have your turn.

PIGGY RAE: Well, that's a relief to me. So far, no one else picked my favorite color, which all of you know anyway because I am famous for this color. Here is my clue:

Number one. This is the color I wore when I competed in the Miss Pork Rind Beauty Contest in 2001.

Number two. This is the color I wore when I sang "The Bellybutton Opera," which I will now perform, free of charge for y'all right now.

[Sing "Bellybutton" to the tune of Handel's "Hallelujah Chorus."]

Bellybutton, bellybutton, bellybutton, bellybutton, belly-but-ton.

Number three. I look gorgeous in this color. Name that color!

SEÑORITA LANA: Piggy Rae. I can see that you put a lot of hard work into this homework assignment. But I'm afraid that I was not present when you won the beauty contest or when you sang that beautiful song. And Piggy Rae, of course you look gorgeous in every color . . . so we need some different clues.

PIGGY RAE: I think most people remember exactly where they were when I was crowned Miss Pork Rind, but I will be nice and give you more clues. Just a minute. I'll be right back. Y'all stay right there.

[Piggy Rae exits, then returns with a pink die-cut of the letter *P* or a large letter *P* written on a piece of paper in pink marker.]

My color starts with the letter *P*, just like this. *P* is also the first letter in Piggy Rae, Pork, and Princess. I always wear this color. It is the color of my feather boa.

SEÑORITA LANA: Piggy Rae's favorite color starts with the letter *P* and is the color of her feather boa. Boys and girls, niños y niñas, de qué color es? Or, what color is this?

[Allow time for audience to say "pink."]

Sí. Yes. It is the color pink. And the Spanish word for pink is rosa (RO sah). Repeat after me: "Rosa."

[Audience repeats:] "Rosa."

Very good! Muy bien! Piggy Rae, did you bring your pink feather boa as a sample of your color?

PIGGY RAE: Yes, and something else, too. [She exits and reenters with a pink rose.] I brought this pink rose to help everyone remember the word rosa.

SEÑORITA LANA: Very good, Piggy Rae! Very Good! Muy bien! Thank you. Gracias. Will you please ask Granny to come here?

PIGGY RAE: Sí. Yes. [Calls out as she exits.] Granny! You're going to have to leave Alistair alone now, because it is your turn!

SEÑORITA LANA: Piggy Rae can be very entertaining, Sí? Granny, will you please come to the front of the class?

GRANNY: [Enters the stage with her back to the audience.] Buenos dias, Señorita Lana. Señorita Lana? Where in tarnation is that teacher?

SEÑORITA LANA: Granny, I'm over here!

[Granny turns around.]

GRANNY: Oh, there you are! Are you trying to fool your old Granny? Well, I've still got some noodles in my head. You can't trick me so easily.

SEÑORITA LANA: We don't wish to trick you, Granny. We just want you to tell us about your favorite color so we can guess what it is.

GRANNY: Well, back in the days when I was just a little girl, when the dinosaurs roamed the earth . . . .

SEÑORITA LANA: Granny!

GRANNY: I'm just kidding. I'm not that old.

SEÑORITA LANA: Granny, let us hear your story about your favorite color.

GRANNY: Well, it's not so much about me, as it is about my grandson, Bernie Bear. Here are my clues; they all rhyme with my favorite color:

Bernie is a sweet little fellow.

He comes to Granny's to eat some Jell-O.

He never makes his Granny bellow,

Because he's really very mellow.

And that is why my favorite col-low [Say to rhyme with yellow.]

Is, in fact, all shades of _____.

SEÑORITA LANA: Boys and girls, niños y niñas, de qué color es? Or, what color is this? What color rhymes with all of Granny's verses? Fellow, bellow, mellow all rhyme with _____?

[Allow time for audience to say "yellow."]

Very good! Muy bien! Granny's favorite color is yellow. The Spanish word for yellow is amarillo (ah mah REE yoh). Repeat after me: "Amarillo."

[Audience repeats:] "Amarillo."

Very good! Muy bien!

Granny, what a lovely rhyme and nice tribute to your grandson, Bernie Bear! Thank you. Gracias.

GRANNY: Hot dog! That was about the best time I've had in the past hundred years or so. I better get back to see if Alistair cleaned up that mess he made in the closet.

SEÑORITA LANA: Adios, Granny!

[Granny exits.]

Boys and girls, niños y niñas, our last student is Mrs. Know-It-All.

MRS. KNOW-IT-ALL: Hello! I'm Mrs. Know-It-All, and I know everything. For example, I know that it is finally my turn.

SEÑORITA LANA: Mrs. Know-It-All, please tell us about your favorite color.

MRS. KNOW-IT-ALL: Listen carefully.

Colors red, orange,

Yellow, green, blue, indigo,

Violet. Lovely.

SEÑORITA LANA: Mrs. Know-It-All! Don't be naughty! You were supposed to give clues, not name your color. And you were supposed to pick only one.

MRS. KNOW-IT-ALL: It was too hard to choose, so I picked these special colors. But it is a clue. My clues make up a distinctive poem, called haiku. Here is another one.

Following the rain,

Colorful arch in the sky

Beautiful to see.

SEÑORITA LANA: Now I understand! Boys and girls, do you know what Mrs. Know-It-All likes the best that has all these colors? It is in the sky after the rain, and it has the colors red, orange, yellow, green, blue, indigo, and violet? Who knows what this is?

[Allow time for audience to respond.]

Sí. Yes. It is the colors of the rainbow. Repeat after me. We will say them all in Spanish.

Red, rojo (ROH hoh).

[Audience repeats:] "Red, rojo."

Orange, anaranjado (ah nah rahn HAH doh).

[Audience repeats:] "Orange, anaranjado."

Yellow, amarillo (ah mah REE yoh).

[Audience repeats:] "Yellow, amarillo."

Green, verde (VAIR deh).

[Audience repeats:] "Green, verde."

Blue, azul (ah SOOL).

[Audience repeats:] "Blue, azul."

Indigo, morado (mo RAH doh).

[Audience repeats:] "Indigo, morado."

Violet, violeta (vee oh LAY tah).

[Audience repeats:] "Violet, violeta."

Very good. Muy bien. And what do you have to show us today, Mrs. Know-It-All?

MRS. KNOW-IT-ALL: I have a picture of a rainbow that I made. I will get it.

[Mrs. Know-It-All exits and returns with the rainbow picture.]

SEÑORITA LANA: That is beautiful. The rainbow. El arcoiris (ahr-koh-EE-rees). And a wonderful way to end our lesson for today. Thank you. Gracias. Good-bye. Adios.

The End

LITERACY TO GO

Dear Parents and Caregivers,

We enjoyed having you and your children attend our storytime today. Today's Literacy To Go tips and book suggestions involve vocabulary, specifically the names of colors.

The puppet show, "My Favorite Colors (Mis Colores Favoritos)" used rhyme, riddles, and poetry to help children guess each puppet's favorite color. At home, you can talk about the colors around you. Teach your children the Spanish names for their favorite colors.

We also introduced color names in Spanish. Use this sheet to help you and your children learn the Spanish names for their favorite colors. We also recommend reading the following books at home with your children.

See you next week.

To listen to a pronunciation guide, try this Web site: www.spanishdict.com/. It has audio capabilities.

Blue = Azul (ah SOOL)

Green = Verde (VAIR deh)

Indigo = Morado (mo RAH doh)

Orange = Anaranjado (ah nah rahn HAH doh)

Pink = Rosa (RO sah)

Red = Rojo (ROH hoh)

Violet = Violeta (vee oh LAY tah)

White = Blanco (BLAHN koh)

Yellow = Amarillo (ah mah REE yoh)

Literacy To Go Take Home Menu

Books that build vocabulary—names of colors:

Board books: Board books are sturdy books that have been specially illustrated for the youngest of readers to enjoy. The following books introduce the world of colors in this easy-to-use format.

Arma, Tom. *Fruity Cutie Colors.*

Boynton, Sandra. *Blue Hat, Green Hat.*
   Also in Spanish: *Azul el Sombrero, Verde el Sombrero.*

Gunzi, Christiane. *My Very First Look at Colors.*

Harrison, Anna. *Colors and Shapes.*

McBratney, Sam. *Colors Everywhere.*

Pfister, Marcus. *Rainbow Fish Colors.*

Rosa-Mendoza, Gladys. *Colors and Shapes (Los Colores y Las Figuras).*

Rubin, Susan Goldman. *Andy Warhol's Colors.*

Schachner, Judith Byron. *Skippyjon Jones: Color Crazy.*

Yannick, Robert. *Red Tractor: A Peek Inside the World of Colors.*

Yolen, Jane. *How Do Dinosaurs Learn Their Colors?*

Picture books

Blackstone, Stella. *Cleo's Color Book.*
Cleo the cat takes a walk outside and discovers colors. A color mixing chart that includes drawings of common items is at the end of the book.

Bullard, Lisa. *Orange Food Fun.*
Books about the colors of the food we eat. See others in the series A+ Books, Eat Your Colors.

Cousins, Lucy. *Maisy's Rainbow Dream.*
Maisy the mouse dreams and sees all the colors of the rainbow. Also in Spanish: *Sueños de Colores Sueños con Maisy.*

Desmazières, Sandra. *Emma and Her Friends: A Book About Colors.*
A girl invites her friends to her birthday party and they talk about their favorite colors.

Dey, Joy Morgan. *Agate: What Good Is a Moose?*
A moose finds good in everyone.

Ehlert, Lois. *Color Farm.*
Bright colors and shapes make learning fun.

Ehlert, Lois. *Color Zoo.*
Identify animals, shapes, and colors.

Ehlert, Lois. *Planting a Rainbow.*
A rainbow of colorful flowers grows in the garden.

Ficocelli, Elizabeth. *Kid Tea.*
If you were kid tea, would your bathwater turn purple after eating grapes?

Gonzalez, Maya Christina. *My Colors, My World. Mis Colores, Mi Mundo.*
A young girl introduces the colors of the desert in English and Spanish.

Horáček, Petr. *Butterfly, Butterfly.*
A little girl follows a butterfly in the garden. Clever cutouts and a surprise at the end.

Jones, Christianne, C. *Big Red Farm.*
Learn about colors and mixing colors to make new colors. See others in the series Know Your Colors.

Kann, Victoria. *Pinkalicious* and *Purplicious.*
The colors pink and purple are delicious!

Kochalka, James. *Squirrelly Gray.*
The adventure begins when a squirrel who lives in a colorless world loses his two front teeth and meets the tooth fairy.

Lopshire, Robert. *Put Me in the Zoo.*
An animal can change colors, go from spots to stripes, and more—all in rhyming verse.

Marks, Jennifer L. *Sorting by Color.*
Jelly beans, toys, socks—how to sort things by color.

Martin, Bill, Jr. *Brown Bear, Brown Bear, What Do You See?*
Classic color story. Great read-aloud. Also in Spanish: *Oso Pardo, Oso Pardo, Que Ves Ahi?.* Translated by Teresa Mlawer.

Rusch, Elizabeth. *A Day with No Crayons.*
A little girl creates art during a day with no crayons.

Seeger, Laura Vaccaro. *Lemons Are Not Red.*
Each page contains a cutout of a familiar shape, and a color it is not—until you turn the page.

Slater, Dashka. *Baby Shoes.*
Written in rhyming verse, baby's new shoes soon become multicolored as he stomps through the park.

Williams, Sue. *I Went Walking*
A boy meets animals of different colors while on a walk. Also in Spanish, *Salí de Paseo.* Translated by Alma F. Ada

English/Spanish first dictionaries: Ask your librarian to help you find the children's Spanish picture dictionaries. Examples are

My First Spanish Picture Dictionary. New York: Barron's, 2001

First Spanish Picture Dictionary. New York: DK Publishing, 2005.

The Usborne Book of Everyday Words in Spanish. London: Usborne Publishing, 1999.

These dictionaries offer engaging photographs of scenes and situations familiar to children, such as a home, a farm, clothing, etc. The pictures are clear and labeled in both English and Spanish. They are excellent choices for vocabulary building in both languages. Pronunciation guides are included.

You're Invited to a
PUPPET SHOW!
Come to storytime and a special puppet show performance of

MY FAVORITE COLORS
(MIS COLORES FAVORITOS)

Piggy Rae loves the color pink. But what about Bernie Bear and Tommy Turtle? What colors do they like best? Using rhymes and riddles, the puppets will give you clues about their favorite colors, and Señorita Lana will also teach us the color names in Spanish.

Our puppet show is specially designed for children ages three through eight and their parents and will help build vocabulary, an important literacy skill.

Date (and day of week): _____

At (library name & address, room number or area)

_____

Let's go! Vamos!

CAUTIOUS TOMMY TURTLE

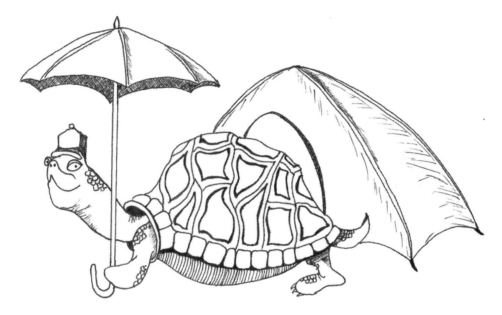

Related Themes: Safety, Turtles, Overcoming fear, Bravery, What if . . .

Overview: Tommy Turtle is prepared for any potential disaster—wind, rain, sunshine, boo-boos—the list goes on. He tells his nephew, Bernie Bear, all about being cautious. Tommy Turtle surprises the audience at the end of the puppet show with the great number of pieces of safety equipment he keeps inside his shell. (This happens offstage, so the objects, of course, are not really inside his shell.) This suspension of belief is the same as the concept behind the Ukrainian folktale, *The Mitten.*

The literacy skill of vocabulary is developed through naming and describing the use of the objects stored inside the turtle's shell.

Early Literacy Skill Focus: The main literacy skill introduced is *vocabulary*, naming objects and describing their purpose. Numerous descriptive words and phrases offer opportunities for vocabulary development. The booklist on the Literacy To Go sheet is rich with titles that reinforce vocabulary development by naming objects and using descriptive phrases.

Other Literacy Opportunities:

- **Vocabulary:** Children develop vocabulary by learning the names of things. They also build vocabulary by using descriptive words to describe nouns. The puppet show lends itself to further exploration of both of these vocabulary-building lessons.

    After the puppet show, use the objects that were presented during the show to allow the children in your audience to name them, as Bernie Bear did. This involves using real things in your storytime. Use descriptive words when talking about their use. For example, you may say, "Look at this yellow nylon windbreaker. It will not keep you warm on a snowy day, because the fabric is so thin. It's called a windbreaker because it keeps strong wind from chilling your skin. That's why Tommy Turtle wanted to take a windbreaker to the park."

You may also discuss the title of the puppet show and the meaning of the word *cautious*.

Tommy Turtle uses the phrases, "Better safe than sorry," and "Look before you leap!" Help your audience explore what these phrases mean.

Materials Needed:

- Puppets: Tommy Turtle, Bernie Bear.

- Props: Tin of bandages, small plastic telescope, water bottle, umbrella, pillow, knee pads, sunscreen bottle (empty and rinsed clean), flashlight, bicycle helmet, map (any road map) cane, windbreaker, scarf, gat, gloves, hand sanitizer bottle (empty and rinsed clean), granola bar.

- Additional safety equipment to decorate Literacy To Go display table—such as an umbrella, a first aid kit, sunglasses, a jacket, a towel, a flashlight, maps, tissues, a sleeping bag, etc.

- Literacy To Go handouts for participants (see pp. 158–59).

- Promotional flyers (see p. 160).

- Display books for checkout; use titles provided on the Literacy To Go handout.

- Titles for read-alouds.

Preparation:

A few weeks or more before the program

- Decide on your storytime theme.
- Announce the storytime program in the library Web site and newsletter.
- Reproduce the promotional flyer (p. 160) and distribute copies to caregivers at the library.

A week or two before the program

- Select and gather your read-aloud titles, as well as display books for checkout, puppets, and props.
- Reproduce the Literacy To Go materials (pp. 158–59).
- Practice the read-aloud books and the puppet play.

On the day of the program

- Create a display of checkout material based on the vocabulary theme nouns and descriptive phrases.
- Include additional safety gear in the Literacy To Go display.

Puppet Show Performance Tips: The humor in this puppet show depends on the audience's understanding that Tommy Turtle's safety equipment is all stored under his shell. When Bernie Bear looks inside Tommy's shell, make it clear that he is really peering under Tommy's shell.

Position the bandage tin and small telescope within easy reach for Bernie to remove. Practice this part a few times to ensure that you can make it work with the puppets that you are using.

Shop around for a turtle puppet that has an empty space between the turtle and its shell.

After you have placed each prop on the stage and Bernie Bear has commented on it, put it back on your side of the stage. Children get very distracted if something falls off the stage in front of them. They are not sure if they should come and pick it up or leave it on the ground.

The Program

During the read-aloud segment: After welcoming the participants, gather the children and caregivers into a semicircle around your storytelling chair. After reading a few books, point out some descriptive words from the read-alouds. Tell the audience that some words describe the things we see. Talk about colors from the picture books you have shared or adjectives such as windy (day), rainy (day), etc. For example, you may say, "We just a read a book about a windy day. What other kinds of words mean windy?" Some words that you might hear will be *breezy, cool wind, blowy.* For younger children you may refer to the puppets. Say, "Turtles have hard shells. Bears have soft fur." Then add some open-ended questions, such as, "What other animals have soft fur?" Reiterate that words like *red* and *yellow*, and *soft* and *hard*, are used to describe the things around us.

Introduce the puppet show: Have the group assemble comfortably around the puppet stage. As leader, address the group with the following welcome.

> I had a great time reading stories to you today. Now, for even more fun, let's do a puppet show! It's called "Cautious Tommy Turtle." Do you know what the word *cautious* means? It means "very careful." Tommy Turtle likes to take things slowly and think things through—very carefully. He wants to be prepared when he takes his nephew, Bernie Bear, to the park. I think you'll be surprised at just how cautious Tommy Turtle can be!

Move to your place behind the puppet stage to begin the show.

After the puppet show: Save enough time after the puppet show to talk about the safety equipment that Tommy Turtle had "inside his shell." During this early literacy discussion to build vocabulary, say the name of the object and some descriptive words such as color words, and *soft* or *shiny*. You may say, "Tommy Turtle had a pair of soft, red, knit mittens under his shell."

Encourage caregivers to checkout the display titles that were selected for the vocabulary enrichment that they offer.

Hand out copies of the Literacy To Go sheet.

Have the puppets tell the children good-bye.

CAUTIOUS TOMMY TURTLE

Puppets:

> Bernie Bear
>
> Tommy Turtle

Props:

> Tin of bandages
>
> Small plastic telescope
>
> Water bottle (empty)
>
> Umbrella
>
> Pillow
>
> Knee pads
>
> Sunscreen bottle (empty and rinsed clean)
>
> Flashlight
>
> Bicycle helmet
>
> Map (any road map)
>
> Cane
>
> Windbreaker
>
> Scarf, hat, and gloves
>
> Hand sanitizer bottle (empty and rinsed clean)
>
> Granola bar

[Enter Bernie Bear.]

BERNIE BEAR: Oh boy, oh boy! I'm so excited! Uncle Tommy told me that he would take me to the park today! I'm so excited! I can hardly wait!

[Enter Tommy Turtle with his head inside his shell.]

BERNIE BEAR: Hi, Uncle Tommy!

TOMMY TURTLE:	Who's that?
BERNIE BEAR:	[Peers inside the shell.] I'm Bernie Bear. Come out and see me.
TOMMY TURTLE:	[Pokes out his head.] Oh, hello. I see you, Bernie Bear. Come and give me a pat on my shell. [Bernie pats Tommy's shell.]
BERNIE BEAR:	Why were you hiding inside your shell?
TOMMY TURTLE:	I wasn't hiding; I was just keeping things tidy. Sometimes it gets crowded inside here, you know, with one thing and another.
BERNIE BEAR:	Really? I don't have a hard shell, so I don't know what it is like to live inside a shell.
TOMMY TURTLE:	Yes, you live in a nice cozy cave with your family. And I live in my nice cozy shell, all by myself.
BERNIE BEAR:	Are you lonely? I would be lonely if I didn't have my mommy and daddy at home.
TOMMY TURTLE:	Not at all. I have everything I need, and I feel very safe. It is important to feel safe.
BERNIE BEAR:	Are you ready to take me to the park now, Uncle Tommy? I've been so excited about it all morning. I can hardly wait!
TOMMY TURTLE:	Well, speaking of feeling safe, I want to make sure that we don't have any accidents at the park. We must be very careful. Do you think that they have mowed the lawn?
BERNIE BEAR:	Mowed the lawn? Why would you worry about tall grass?
TOMMY TURTLE:	I'm very short. When the grass is too high, I cannot see over the top of it. We could get lost in a tall grass jungle.
BERNIE BEAR:	Don't worry. I'm a very, very, very big bear boy and I can see over tall grass. I saw my daddy mow the lawn. I think that I could push a lawnmower. I'm a very, very, very big bear boy!
TOMMY TURTLE:	Oh dear! Lawnmowers are so loud! If you use a lawnmower, you need some earplugs to keep your eardrums safe. You wouldn't want to ruin your hearing. Hmmm, I think I better find a periscope

for my "better safe than sorry" kit, and then I'll be able to see over the tall grass.

BERNIE BEAR: What is a pe-ri-scope?

TOMMY TURTLE: It's a special safety device that they use on boats called submarines. It goes way up, above the water, so they can look around. I can use one to see over tall grass.

BERNIE BEAR: Oh yeah, I saw them use a periscope in a movie. Hey, can you boys and girls say that new word after me? Say "pe-ri-scope."
[Audience says:] "Periscope."

BERNIE BEAR: That's right. Periscope.

TOMMY TURTLE: That settles it; I'm going to buy a periscope.

BERNIE BEAR: Okay. When we get to the park we can play submarines! I'm going to be a big, grey underwater submarine and use my pe-ri-scope to see over the tall grass. Can we play submarines, Uncle Tommy?

TOMMY TURTLE: Ohhhh, dear. What did you say about underwater?

BERNIE BEAR: We can pretend that we are underwater and use our periscopes to see each other.

TOMMY TURTLE: I wonder where I can find a submarine. We could use one in case it rains and rains and then it floods and then we need a submarine with a periscope to find our way home. Ohhhh, dear!

BERNIE BEAR: It won't rain. Look at the sky. It's a beautiful, sunny day!
[They both look up at the sky.]

BERNIE BEAR: See! I just wanted to play a pretend underwater submarine game. But if you are worried about rain, I can put an umbrella in my backpack.

TOMMY TURTLE: There's no need for you to bring a backpack. I'll just put an umbrella in my "better safe than sorry" kit. Ohhhh, wait! I just felt a breeze! Did you feel that breeze? What if it gets too windy?

BERNIE BEAR: C'mon, Uncle Tommy. It was just a little breeze. I'll wear my windbreaker. It'll be okay. Let's walk to the park. I really, really, really want to go play in the park.

TOMMY TURTLE: Okay, but I'm staying inside my shell. [Pulls his head inside his shell.] That'll keep me out of harm's way.

[Tommy walks along with his head inside the shell. He goes the wrong way and bumps into the side of the puppet stage.]

Ouch! What was that? [Peeks out.]

BERNIE BEAR: Uncle Tommy, you're going the wrong way!

TOMMY TURTLE: Ouch. Well, see, that's a good lesson for you. Don't go on a walk if you have your head inside your shell. It's not safe. That's why they say, "Look before you leap!" [Puts head out completely.] That means that you should plan ahead before you do something. Oh, no, I just had a terrible thought! What if you get boo-boos and don't have bandages? Ohhhh, dear. [He exits.]

BERNIE BEAR: Uncle Tommy! Where are you going?

TOMMY TURTLE: [Reenters.] I needed to put an umbrella, a windbreaker, and some bandages inside my "better safe than sorry" kit.

BERNIE BEAR: I get it. You need an umbrella in case it rains, a windbreaker in case the wind blows too hard, and some bandages in case I get a boo-boo. Uncle Tommy, you're the best uncle. You think of everything.

TOMMY TURTLE: I like to be prepared so I don't have to worry. And while I was walking around with my head inside my shell, I thought about how dark it is inside there. And I thought, "What if we were having so much fun at the park that we forgot the time of day, and the sun set, and it started to get dark, and we got lost wandering around late at night, and . . . oh dear!"

BERNIE BEAR: That's true.

TOMMY TURTLE: So I better put a flashlight and a map in my "better safe than sorry" kit. And I need a telescope and map of the sky in case we have to navigate by the stars.

BERNIE BEAR: Uncle Tommy, we're only going to the park, we're not sailing around the world!

TOMMY TURTLE: Well, I like to be prepared. Wait here, and I'll gather some basic safety equipment before we walk to the park. [He exits.]

BERNIE BEAR: Hurry, Uncle Tommy! I want to go play at the park!

TOMMY TURTLE: Okay then. I have everything that I could find. I guess we're ready to walk to the park.

BERNIE BEAR: Oh, goody! Thanks Uncle Tommy. I'm so excited.

TOMMY TURTLE: We better get started. We need to be cautious and careful. You never know what might happen. That's why I have my "better safe than sorry" kit.

BERNIE BEAR: Roger that, Uncle Tommy.

TOMMY TURTLE: What did you say?

BERNIE BEAR: I said, "Roger that." You know, I was pretending that I we had walkie-talkies and that we were policemen and we were talking to each other.

TOMMY TURTLE: Walkie-talkies. Those would be good to have for an emergency. Then I wouldn't have to worry because you run so much faster than I can. We can always stay in touch with a walkie-talkie. I'm going to have to find some walkie-talkies to put in my "better safe than sorry" kit.

BERNIE BEAR: Hey, Uncle Tommy. Do you want to see how fast I can run? Look at me run! [He "runs" off the stage, and Tommy Turtle turns around slowly to watch him run. Before he can turn all the way around, Bernie Bear reenters the stage, panting.]

[Pant, pant.] See how fast I am? I'm a big, big, big bear boy and a fast, fast, fast big bear boy!

TOMMY TURTLE: You are fast, Bernie Bear. I'm proud of you. But you have to promise me that you won't run to the park. I want you to stay right beside me, and we'll look both ways before we cross the street.

BERNIE BEAR: Roger that, Uncle Tommy.

[Tommy Turtle and Bernie Bear exit. While you have them offstage, put the tin of bandages and the small plastic telescope inside Tommy Turtle's shell.]

[Puppets return to stage. They start walking together slowly. Pause.]

BERNIE BEAR:	Uncle Tommy?
TOMMY TURTLE:	Yes, Bernie Bear?
BERNIE BEAR:	You seem to be walking slower than usual.
TOMMY TURTLE:	I'm carrying a lot of equipment in my "better safe than sorry" kit.
BERNIE BEAR:	I was wondering about that. You talked so much about your "better safe than sorry" kit . . . .
TOMMY TURTLE:	Yes?
BERNIE BEAR:	Well, aren't you going to bring it with us? Where is it?
TOMMY TURTLE:	Oh, I have it with me at all times. I keep my "better safe than sorry" kit very safe and close.
BERNIE BEAR:	I don't see it.
TOMMY TURTLE:	That because it's under my shell.
BERNIE BEAR:	Under your shell?
TOMMY TURTLE:	Oh, yes. I keep all my emergency supplies right under my shell.
BERNIE BEAR:	Let me see! I want to see! Uncle Tommy, let me see.
TOMMY TURTLE:	Go right ahead. [Bernie gets down on his side and peers into Tommy's shell.]
BERNIE BEAR:	Oh, my goodness! There is a lot of stuff in there.
TOMMY TURTLE:	It's not just stuff. It's everything you might need in case of an emergency.
BERNIE BEAR:	Oh, I see the bandages that you just put in there. [He reaches into Tommy Turtle's shell and pulls out the tin of bandages.]
TOMMY TURTLE:	Yep, there are the bandages. Because what if you fall and skin your knee? I'll be prepared.
BERNIE BEAR:	Oh, look at this! Here's the telescope to help you see when you have to navigate using the stars!

TOMMY TURTLE: Yes, indeed. It's best to be prepared. I'd rather be better safe than sorry. That's why I call it my "better safe than sorry" kit.

BERNIE BEAR: [Keeps looking in Tommy Turtle's shell.] Holy cow! There's a lot of safety equipment in here. Can you show me what else you have under your shell?

TOMMY TURTLE: You mean you want to see everything that I have in my "better safe than sorry" kit? Well, you know, I'm a little shy. And all of the boys and girls are watching. Maybe I should hide behind the curtain while I take out all my safety gear. But get ready, because I have a lot of safety equipment.

BERNIE BEAR: Really? Let me see. I want to see what you have.

[Tommy Turtle exits and at this point the puppeteer has Tommy Turtle return with each prop, one at a time, and hold it for the audience to see while Bernie Bear names it.]

Hey, boys and girls, I have an idea. Uncle Tommy is going to show us what he keeps under his shell, in his "better safe than sorry" kit. When he shows us his stuff, I will tell you what it is, and then you say it after me. We already saw some bandages. [Bernie exits and gets the bandages and holds them up for the audience to see.] So, I'll say bandages, and then you repeat it. "Bandages."

[Audience repeats:] "Bandages."

Good job. Those are in case I get a boo-boo.

[He gets the telescope.]

"Telescope."

[Audience repeats:] "Telescope."

That's in case we get lost at night, we can use a telescope to see the stars.

TOMMY TURTLE: I'm ready. I have all my safety stuff out of my shell for you to see.

BERNIE BEAR: We're ready for you to show us what you had in your "better safe than sorry" kit.

[Tommy Turtle enters with water bottle.]

Okay, kids, here we go. A water bottle.

[Audience repeats:] "Water bottle."

TOMMY TURTLE: Just in case we get thirsty. [He exits and reenters with an umbrella.]

BERNIE BEAR: "Umbrella."

[Audience repeats:] "Umbrella."

TOMMY TURTLE: In case it rains. [He exits and reenters with a pillow.]

BERNIE BEAR: "Pillow."

[Audience repeats:] "Pillow."

TOMMY TURTLE: Just in case you go down the slide at the playground and fall on your bottom.

BERNIE BEAR: Or, what if we get lost in the wilderness and have to spend the night?

TOMMY TURTLE: Ohhhh, dear! I never thought of that! Maybe I should put a sleeping bag inside my "better safe than sorry" kit.

BERNIE BEAR: I would have fun spending the night in the wilderness with you, Uncle Tommy. But what else do you keep under your shell?

TOMMY TURTLE: I'll show you. [He exits and reenters with knee pads.]

BERNIE BEAR: "Knee pads."

[Audience repeats:] "Knee pads."

TOMMY TURTLE: Just in case you fall. [He exits and reenters with a an empty sunscreen bottle that has been rinsed clean.]

BERNIE BEAR: "Sunscreen."

[Audience repeats:] "Sunscreen."

TOMMY TURTLE: Just in case the sun shines. [He exits and reenters with a flashlight.]

BERNIE BEAR: "Flashlight."

[Audience repeats:] "Flashlight."

TOMMY TURTLE: In case we have to find our way home after dark.

BERNIE BEAR: Are you sure you had all this stuff under your shell?

TOMMY TURTLE: Yes, it was very cozy in here. But wait, there's more . . . . [He exits and reenters with a bicycle helmet.]

BERNIE BEAR: "Bicycle helmet."

[Audience repeats:] "Bicycle helmet."

TOMMY TURTLE: Just in case you ride your bike. [He exits and reenters with a map.]

BERNIE BEAR: "Map."

[Audience repeats:] "Map."

TOMMY TURTLE: So we can always find the right road home. [He exits and reenters with a cane.]

BERNIE BEAR: "Cane."

[Audience repeats:] "Cane."

TOMMY TURTLE: Just in case you sprain your ankle. [He exits and reenters with a windbreaker.]

BERNIE BEAR: "Windbreaker."

[Audience repeats:] "Windbreaker.'

TOMMY TURTLE: Just in case you get stuck in a windstorm. [He exits and reenters with a scarf, hat and gloves. Bring up separately, if necessary.]

BERNIE BEAR: "Scarf, hat, and gloves."

[Audience repeats:] "Scarf, hat, and gloves."]

TOMMY TURTLE: Just in case you get stuck in a snowstorm. [He exits and reenters with an empty hand cleaner bottle that has been rinsed clean].

BERNIE BEAR: "Hand cleaner."

[Audience repeats:] "Hand cleaner."

TOMMY TURTLE: Just in case you get germs. [He exits and reenters with a granola bar.]

BERNIE BEAR: "Granola bar."

[Audience repeats:] "Granola bar."

TOMMY TURTLE: Just in case you need a healthy snack.

BERNIE BEAR: Whew! Uncle Tommy! That's a lot of being prepared! Did you really have all that stuff under your shell? I bet you could hardly move!

TOMMY TURTLE: That's okay. Turtles like to take it slow and easy. We like to be careful and cautious. And I like safety first!

BERNIE BEAR: I have another question for you, Uncle Tommy.

TOMMY TURTLE: Yes, Bernie Bear?

BERNIE BEAR: Have you ever thought, "What if it we had a beautiful sunny day and we had tons of fun. What if NOTHING went wrong?"

TOMMY TURTLE: Ohhhh, dear. I never thought of that! I better start to prepare for the perfect day.

[They exit.]

The End

LITERACY TO GO

Dear Parents and Caregivers,

Thank you for coming to storytime today. In our puppet show, "Cautious Tommy Turtle," Tommy Turtle wanted to make sure that Bernie Bear didn't get hurt at the park, so he stored safety equipment in his "better safe than sorry" kit under his turtle shell. We named the equipment and used descriptive words to talk about it.

You can start at a very young age naming things to your child—for example, the food that you are feeding your baby, a dish, a spoon, and so forth. Continue adding more complex words to your everyday speech as your child grows older.

Children's books introduce new words for children in a fun and colorful way. The books listed below are rich with new vocabulary words and descriptive phrases. You'll enjoy reading them with your child.

See you next week!

Literacy To Go Take Home Menu

Books that build vocabulary: These books introduce descriptive words and phrases.

The 20th Century Children's Book Treasury. Selected by Janet Schulman.
> Contains a wealth of exceptional vocabulary-building children's literature.

Brett, Jan. *The Mitten: A Ukrainian Folktale.*
> Name the animals who manage to squeeze into a knitted white mitten.

Cronin, Doreen. *Click, Clack, Moo: Cows that Type.*
> The cows type letters to the farmer demanding better living conditions.

Ehlert, Lois. *Snowballs.*
> You and your child will be entertained for hours naming all the items used to make snowmen, snow-women, snow-babies, and more.

Elting, Mary. *Q Is for Duck: An Alphabet Guessing Game*
> Q is for duck because a duck says "Quack," and other unconventional alphabet riddles.

Emmett, Jonathan. *Through the Heart of the Jungle.*
> A cumulative rhyme that incorporates different words for eating.

Hindley, Judy. *Baby Talk : A Book of First Words and Phrases.*
> The words a baby uses while talking about his day.

Johnson, David *Snow Sounds: An Onomatopoeic Story.*
> *Crunch, jingly, scrape* . . . words describe a snowy wonderland.

Menchin, Scott. *Taking a Bath with the Dog and Other Things That Make Me Happy.*
> Various people describe what makes them happy.

Meyers, Susan. *Kittens! Kittens! Kittens!*
> From being a kitten to having kittens of their own, read about the lives of pouncing, bouncing kittens.

From *Puppet Plays Plus: Using Stock Characters to Entertain and Teach Early Literacy* by Laurel L. Iakovakis. Westport, CT: Libraries Unlimited. Copyright © 2009.

Moss, Miriam. *Bare Bear.*
> A bare bear goes on a funny adventure while looking for his striped sock.

O'Connor, Jane. *Fancy Nancy*; *Fancy Nancy and the Posh Puppy*; and *Fancy Nancy's Favorite Fancy Words: From Accessories to Zany.*
> Nancy dresses fancy and talks fancy in the glittery pages of these books.

Prince, April Jones. *What Do Wheels Do All Day?*
> Names objects that have wheels—cars, wheelchairs, etc.

Rosen, Michael. *We're Going on a Bear Hunt.*
> Going on a bear hunt, and along the way, they climb a grassy slope, swish across a river, and sludge through the mud.

Scieszka, Jon. *The Stinky Cheese Man and Other Fairly Stupid Tales.*
> Funny stories, loaded with descriptive words.

Shore, Diane Z. *Look Both Ways: A Cautionary Tale.*
> Accidents happen! Be careful.

Sperring, Mark. *Mermaid Dreams.*
> Descriptive beach and ocean words in a sweet mermaid story.

Tafuri, Nancy. *The Busy Little Squirrel.*
> Squirrel is busy—he has no time to nibble, hop, or run.

Viorst, Judith. *Absolutely Positively Alexander: Alexander, the Complete Stories.*
> Contains the Alexander stories, including *Alexander and the Terrible, Horrible, No Good, Very Bad Day.*

Wood, Audrey. *The Napping House.*
> It was a quiet, sleepy house until a wakeful flea happened along.

Yolen, Jane. *Sleep, Black Bear, Sleep.*
> A cozy, comforting tale that explores other words for sleep—*doze, nod, dream*—with droopy-eyed creatures snuggling up in their warm dens while it snows outside.

You're Invited to a PUPPET SHOW!
Come to storytime and a special puppet show performance of

CAUTIOUS TOMMY TURTLE

Bernie Bear wants Tommy Turtle to take him to the park. Tommy is worried that it might rain, it might be windy, and it might even be too sunny. He should take an umbrella, a windbreaker, sunglasses, and more . . . just in case! Can you ever be overly prepared?

Join us for this fun puppet play with a surprise ending. The books that we read at storytime introduce your child to words that they generally do not hear on television or in everyday conversations. Building a good vocabulary is an important early literacy skill.

Our puppet show is specially designed for children ages three through eight and their parents.

Date (and day of week): _____

At (library name & address, room number or area)

_____

APPENDIX: LITERACY SKILL BIBLIOGRAPHIES

The following bibliographies come from the Literacy To Go handouts. Use these titles for display, readers' advisory, and literacy skill development. Providing easy access to books that enhance the early literacy skill that you have talked about at your storytime encourages caregivers to model your behavior at home.

Phonological Awareness

Using Animal Sounds

These books invite participation and interaction through mimicking animal sounds.
Booklist from "Mrs. Know-It-All Game Show: Who Says That?"

Baddiel, Ivor, and Sophie Jubb. *Cock-a-Doodle Quack! Quack!* Oxford, New York: David Fickling Books, 2007.
> Baby rooster learns how to say cock-a-doodle-doo!

Beil, Karen Magnuson. *Mooove Over!: A Book About Counting by Twos.* New York: Holiday House, 2004.
> A noisy cow wants more space to herself, so she tells the other animals to "mooove over!"

Butler, John. *Can You Growl Like a Bear?* Atlanta, GA: Peachtree, 2007.
> Each page invites the readers to make an animal sound.

Cronin, Doreen. *Dooby Dooby Moo.* New York: Atheneum Books for Young Readers, 2006.
> With much revelry, farm animals compete in a talent show.

Dallas-Conté, Julie. *Cock-a-Moo-Moo.* Boston: Little, Brown, 2001.
> A rooster get help from the barnyard animals to remember how to cock-a-doodle-doo.

Davis, Katie. *Who Hoots?* Orlando, FL.: Voyager Books/Harcourt, 2004, 2000.
> Who buzzes, squeaks, roars, and quacks?

DiPucchio, Kelly S. *What's the Magic Word?* New York: HarperCollins, 2005.
> A cow thinks the magic word is "moo"; a pig says it's "oink." What is the magic word?

Fleming, Denise. *The Cow Who Clucked.* New York: Henry Holt, 2006.
> The cow looks for everywhere for her lost "moo".

Godwin, Laura. *What the Baby Hears.* New York: Hyperion Books for Children, 2002.
> Baby bear hears grr, grr, grr; kitten hears purr, purr, purr.

Kuskin, Karla. *Roar and More*. Honesdale, PA: Boyds Mills Press, 2004, 1990.
This book will make you roar, hiss, and more.

Kutner, Merrily. *Down on the Farm*. New York: Holiday House, 2004.
A noisy, active farmyard adventure.

Lawrence, John. *This Little Chick*. Cambridge, MA: Candlewick Press, 2002.
An entertaining little chick learns to talk to the animals in their own language.

MacDonald, Margaret Read. *A Hen, a Chick, and a String Guitar*. Cambridge, MA: Barefoot Books, 2005.
A musical story with animal sounds.

Martin, Bill, Jr. *Polar Bear, Polar Bear, What Do You Hear?* New York: Henry Holt, 1991.
A popular and much-loved animal sound story.

McGee, Marni. *The Noisy Farm: Lots of Animal Noises to Enjoy!* New York: Bloomsbury Children's Books, 2004.
And lots of animal sounds to mimic!

Most, Bernard. *The Cow That Went Oink*. San Diego: Red Wagon Books; Harcourt Brace & Company, 2003, 1990.
A classic moo and oink story.

Murphy, Yannick. *Ahwoooooooo!* New York: Clarion Books, 2006.
Help teach a wolf to howl at the moon.

Palatini, Margie. *Moo, Who?* New York: Katherine Tegen Books, c2004.
After an accident with a flying cow pie, a cow forgets what she is supposed to say.

Parenteau, Shirley. *One Frog Sang*. Cambridge, MA: Candlewick Press, 2007.
A counting story with many ways to mimic frog sounds.

Pedersen, Janet. *Millie Wants to Play*. Cambridge, MA: Candlewick Press, 2004.
A baby calf and her friends wake up before the rooster crows.

Polacco, Patricia. *Mommies Say Shhh!* New York: Philomel Books, 2005.
An active farmyard, but mommy holds baby quietly, saying, "Shhh."

Prap, Lila, 1955. *Animals speak*. New York: North-South Books, 2006.
Describes how other languages "translate" animal sounds.

Taylor, Thomas. *The Loudest Roar*. New York: Arthur A. Levine Books, 2002.
A small tiger startles his jungle friends with his roar.

Walton, Rick. *Herd of Cows! Flock of Sheep! Quiet! I'm Tired! I Need My Sleep!* Salt Lake City: Gibbs Smith, 2002.
The farmer is so sleepy that even the most raucous of animals can't seem to wake him up.

Whybrow, Ian. *The Noisy Way to Bed*. New York: Arthur A. Levine Books, 2004.
Just before the reader says the word *bed*, a noisy animal interrupts.

Repetitive Text

The following books have a refrain that is repeated throughout. Booklist from "Moosterpiece Theater: Clever Piggy Rae and the Big Bad Wolf."

Anderson, Peggy Perry. *Joe on the Go.* Boston: Houghton Mifflin, 2007.
> Joe wants to play and finally finds someone who wants to play with him—Grandma.

Aylesworth, Jim. *Little Bitty Mousie.* New York: Walker; distributed to the trade by Holtzbrinck Publishers, 2007.
> A mouse sniffs her way through the alphabet.

Emberley, Ed. *Go Away, Big Green Monster!* Boston: Little, Brown, 1992.
> Strategically cut out pages make this fun story an adventurous page-turner.

Fleming, Denise. *The Cow Who Clucked.* New York: Henry Holt, 2006.
> A cow looking for her moo discovers, "It is not you who has my moo!" Where will she find it?

Gerritsen, Paula. *Nuts.* Asheville, NC: Front Street, 2006.
> A minimal amount of text is used to describe a tiny mouse gathering nuts for the winter.

Gerstein, Mordicai. *Leaving the Nest.* New York: Farrar, Straus & Giroux, 2007.
> A bevy of backyard animals watch a baby blue jay take flight.

Harper, Anita. *It's Not Fair!* New York: Holiday House, 2007.
> It's not fair that baby brother gets away with so much. It's not fair that big sister gets to do so much.

Hennessy, B[arbara] G. *The Boy Who Cried Wolf.* New York: Simon & Schuster Books for Young Readers, 2006.
> An Aesop fable, retold with a strong lesson, descriptive words, and wonderful illustrations.

Martin, Bill, Jr. *Brown Bear, Brown Bear, What Do You See?* New York: Henry Holt, 1983.
> Each animal is asked the same refrain. A modern classic; a must read.

Mayr, Diane. *Run, Turkey, Run.* New York: Walker, 2007.
> It is Thanksgiving time, and the turkey had better run, turkey, run!

Meyers, Susan. *Kittens! Kittens! Kittens!* New York: Abrams Books for Young Readers, 2007.

Meyers, Susan. *Puppies! Puppies! Puppies!* New York: Abrams Books for Young Readers, 2005.
> Easy to read yet descriptive. Repeats title throughout each book.

Parker, Marjorie Blain. *Your Kind of Mommy.* New York: Dutton Children's Books, c2007.
> Animal mommies and people mommies love their babies

Rosen, Michael. *Bear's Day Out.* New York: Bloomsbury Children's Books; distributed to the trade by Holtzbrinck Publishers, 2007.
> Many repeatable refrains are used to describe Bear's adventure, from a cave to the city.

Scieszka, Jon [with help from David Shannon, Loren Long, and David Gordon]. *Smash! Crash!* London: Simon & Schuster Children's, 2008.
> There will be no stopping the children from repeating "Smash! Crash!"

Shannon, David. *Good Boy, Fergus!* New York: Blue Sky Press, 2006.
Fergus is not the most well-behaved dog, but he's certainly cute.

Shapiro, Jody Fickes. *Family Lullaby.* New York: Greenwillow Books, c2007.
Parents, grandparents, everyone loves baby.

Sherry, Kevin. *I'm the Biggest Thing in the Ocean.* New York: Dial Books for Young Readers, 2007.
A giant squid thinks he is the biggest thing in the ocean.

Shulevitz, Uri. *So Sleepy Story.* New York: Farrar, Straus & Giroux, 2006.
Everything in the house is "so sleepy."

Sillifant, Alec. *Farmer Ham.* New York: North-South Books, 2007.
Farmer Ham can't seem to scare away crows.

Squires, Janet. *The Gingerbread Cowboy.* New York: HarperCollins, 2006.
"Giddyup, giddyup as fast as you can. You can't catch me, I'm the Gingerbread Man!"

Stainton, Sue. *I Love Cats.* New York: Katherine Tegen Books, 2007.
If you love cats, you'll love this book.

Stoeke, Janet Morgan. *The Bus Stop.* New York: Dutton Children's Books, 2007.
School bus ride instills confidence in children.

Tafuri, Nancy. *The Busy Little Squirrel.* New York: Simon & Schuster Books for Young Readers, 2007.
A busy squirrel gathers food for the winter.

Weaver, Tess. *Cat Jumped In!* New York: Clarion Books, 2007.
Cat jumps in through a window and into a closet; where next?

Wilson, Karma. *Bear Snores On.* New York: Margaret K. McElderry Books, 2001.
Bear hibernates and nothing (maybe) wakes him up.

Wilson, Karma. *Bear Wants More.* New York: Margaret K. McElderry Books, 2003.
The bear from *Bear Snores On* wakes up from his hibernation, and he is hungry!

Wilson, Karma. *Princess Me.* New York: Margaret K. McElderry Books, 2007.
Perfect read-aloud for princesses.

Wood, Audrey. *King Bidgood's in the Bathtub.* San Diego: Harcourt Brace Jovanovich, 1985.
Will anyone be able to figure out how to get the king out of the tub?

Wood, Audrey. *Silly Sally.* San Diego: Harcourt Brace Jovanovich, 1992.
This cumulative story invites a rhythmical sing along.

Zimmerman, Andrea Griffing. *Dig!* Orlando: Silver Whistle, 2004.
A counting rhyme at a construction site.

Rhyming Text

Rhyming words and rhythmical verse help to build phonological awareness. Booklist from "Piggy Rae Meets Her Neighbors."

Anderson, Peggy Perry. *Let's Clean Up!* Boston: Houghton Mifflin, 2002
A frog tries to clean up his room, but it's not to Mother's satisfaction.

Dodds, Dayle Ann. *The Prince Won't Go to Bed!* New York: Farrar, Straus & Giroux, 2007.
What will it take to get the prince to go to bed?

Edwards, David. *The Pen That Pa Built.* Berkeley, CA: Tricycle Press, 2007.
A rhyming book that celebrates farming and raising sheep.

Falwell, Cathryn. *Scoot!* New York: Greenwillow Books, 2008.
While other pond animals glide and dash and splash, the turtles sit quietly—like stones.

Falwell, Cathryn. *Shape Capers.* New York: Greenwillow Books, 2007.
Learn your shapes, and use your imagination to see what can be built from them.

Goldstone, Bruce. *The Beastly Feast.* New York: Henry Holt, 1998.
Hungry animals bring their favorite foods to a feast.

Greene, Rhonda Gowler. *This Is the Teacher.* New York: Dutton Children's Books, 2004.
Written along the lines of "This is the house that Jack built," this is the story of a teacher's day and her active classroom.

Hindley, Judy. *Baby Talk* Cambridge, MA: Candlewick Press, 2006
Rhyming verse follows baby's activities throughout the day.

Hubbell, Patricia. *Firefighters! Speeding! Spraying! Saving!* Tarrytown, NY: Marshall Cavendish, 2007.
A rhyming story about brave firefighters, with colorful pictures and vivid verse.

McHenry, E. B. *Has Anyone Seen Winnie and Jean?* New York: Bloomsbury Children's Books; distributed to the trade by Holtzbrinck Publishers, 2007.
Two little dogs, Winnie and Jean, escape from their yard and have an adventure, with the police hot on their trail.

Mitton, Tony. *Down by the Cool of the Pool.* New York: Orchard Books, 2002.
This book will have you singing and clapping.

Postgate, Daniel. *Engelbert Sneem and His Dream Vacuum Machine.* New York: North-South Books, 2007, 2006.
Engelbert uses his vacuum to suck up children's dreams and take them home to watch them himself. Imaginative.

Ryder, Joanne. *Won't You Be My Hugaroo?* New York: Harcourt, 2006.
A comforting book all about hugs.

Sierra, Judy. *Preschool to the Rescue.* San Diego: Gulliver Books, Harcourt Brace, 2001.
Preschoolers help to rescue a police car, tow truck, and more.

Ward, Jennifer. *Over in the Garden.* Flagstaff, AZ: Rising Moon, 2002.
A garden bug version of *Over in the Meadow.*

Weeks, Sarah. *Bunny Fun*. Orlando, FL: Harcourt, 2006.
A bunny and a mouse have a mischievous day.

Wilcox, Leah. *Waking Beauty*. New York: G.P. Putnam Sons, 2008.
Sleeping Beauty is snoring. How is the prince to awaken her?

Wilson, Karma. *Frog in the Bog*. New York: Margaret K. McElderry Books, c2003.
A rhyming and counting book about a frog with a big appetite.

Wilson, Karma. *Moose Tracks* New York: Margaret K. McElderry Books, c2006.
A messy house and a messy yard are easily explained. But who left the moose tracks?

Yolen, Jane. *Dimity Duck*. New York: Philomel Books, 2006.
Dimity Duck has a fun day with her friend, Frumity Frog.

Singing

These books contain the words to popular songs. You may sing them as you read them. You'll also enjoy the colorful illustrations. Booklist from "Bedtime for Bernie Bear."

Bates, Ivan. *Five Little Ducks*. New York: Scholastic, 2006.

Cabrera, Jane. *Ten in the Bed*. New York: Holiday House, 2006.

Canyon, Christopher. *John Denver's Take Me Home, Country Roads*. Nevada City, CA: Dawn Publications, 2005.

Montgomery, Wayne. *Over the Candlestick: Classic Nursery Rhymes and the Real Stories Behind Them*. Atlanta, GA: Peachtree Publishers, 2002

Nursery Songs and Lullabies. Featuring the art of Bessie Pease Gutmann. New York: Grosset & Dunlap, 2007.

Pinkney, J Brian. *Hush Little Baby*. New York: Greenwillow Books, c2006.

Trapani, Iza. *Baa Baa Black Sheep*. Watertown, MA: Whispering Coyote Press, 2001.

Trapani, Iza. *Froggie Went A-Courtin'*. Watertown, MA: Charlesbridge, 2002.

Trapani, Iza. *Here We Go 'Round the Mulberry Bush*. Watertown, MA: Charlesbridge, 2006.

Trapani, Iza. *I'm a Little Teapot*. Watertown, MA: Whispering Coyote Press, 1996.

Trapani, Iza. *The Itsy Bitsy Spider*. Watertown, MA: Charlesbridge, 1993.

Trapani, Iza. *Oh Where, Oh Where Has My Little Dog Gone?* Watertown, MA: Charlesbridge, 1995.

Trapani, Iza. *Row, Row, Row Your Boat*. Dallas, TX: Whispering Coyote Press, 1999.

Trapani, Iza. *Shoo Fly!* Watertown, MA: Charlesbridge, 2000.

Trapani, Iza. *Twinkle, Twinkle Little Star*. Dallas, TX: Whispering Coyote Press, 1994.

Warhola, James. *If You're Happy and You Know It*. New York: Orchard Books, 2007.

Yarrow, Pete and Leonard Lipton. *Puff, the Magic Dragon*. New York: Sterling, 2007.

<u>Traditional Songs</u> (series). Edited by Ann Owen. Minneapolis, MN: Picture Window Books, 2003. Titles include:

The Ants Go Marching

Clementine

The Farmer in the Dell

I Know an Old Lady

I've Been Working on the Railroad

She'll Be Coming Around the Mountain

Vocabulary

Names of Colors

Because this category involves concepts, two separate lists are included, one for board books and one for picture books. Caregivers of very young children appreciate concept books in board book format. To further reinforce the lesson presented in the puppet show, some Spanish books are also included. Booklist from "My Favorite Colors (Mis Colores Favoritos)."

Board Books

The following books introduce the world of colors in an easy-to-use format.

Arma, Tom. *Fruity Cutie Colors.* New York: Abrams, 2004.

Boynton, Sandra. *Azul el Sombrero, Verde el Sombrero.* New York: Simon & Schuster Libros Para Niños, 1984, 1995.

Boynton, Sandra. *Blue Hat, Green Hat.* New York: Little Simon, 1984.

Gunzi, Christiane. *My Very First Look at Colors.* Minnetonka, MN: Two-Can Publishing, 2006.

Harrison, Anna. *Colors and Shapes.* London, New York: DK Publishing, 2007

Hill, Eric. *Spot's Colors, Shapes and Numbers.* New York: G. P. Putnam's Sons, 2007.

McBratney, Sam. *Colors Everywhere.* Cambridge, MA: Candlewick Press, 2008.

Pfister, Marcus. *Rainbow Fish Colors.* New York: North-South Books, 2004.

Rosa-Mendoza, Gladys. *Colors and Shapes; Los Colores y Las Figuras.* Wheaton, IL: me+mi publishing, 2000.

Rubin, Susan Goldman. *Andy Warhol's Colors.* San Francisco: Chronicle Books, 2007.

Schachner, Judith Byron. *Skippyjon Jones: Color Crazy.* New York: Dutton Children's Books, 2007.

Yannick, Robert. *Red Tractor: A Peek Inside the World of Colors.* Golden Books, 2006.

Yolen, Jane. *How Do Dinosaurs Learn Their Colors?* New York: Blue Sky Press, 2006.

Picture Books

Learn color names through literature.

Bullard, Lisa. *Orange Food Fun*. Mankato, MN: Capstone Press, 2006.
Books about the colors of the food we eat. See others in this series, <u>A+ Books,</u> <u>Eat Your</u> <u>Colors</u>.

Cousins, Lucy. *Maisy's Rainbow Dream*. Cambridge, MA: Candlewick Press, 2003.
Maisy the mouse dreams and sees all the colors of the rainbow. Also in Spanish: *Sueños de Colores Sueños con Maisy*.

Desmazières, Sandra. *Emma and Her Friends: A Book About Colors*. Milwaukee, MN: Gareth Stevens Publishers, 2007.
A girl invites her friends to her birthday party, and they talk about their favorite colors.

Dey, Joy Morgan. *Agate: What Good Is a Moose?* Duluth, MN: Lake Superior Port Cities Inc, 2007.
A moose finds good in everyone.

Ehlert, Lois. *Color Farm*. New York: HarperCollins, 1990.

Ehlert, Lois. *Color Zoo*. New York: HarperCollins, 1989.
Clever use of shapes and colors.

Ehlert, Lois. *Planting a Rainbow*. San Diego: Harcourt Brace Jovanovich, 1988.
A rainbow of colorful flowers grows in the garden.

Ficocelli, Elizabeth. *Kid Tea*. Tarrytown, NY: Marshall Cavendish, 2007.
If you were kid tea, would your bathwater turn purple after eating grapes?

First Spanish Picture Dictionary. New York: DK Publishing, 2005.
Clear, labeled pictures of locations and situations familiar to children. Great vocabulary booster for both English and Spanish.

Gonzalez, Maya Christina. *My Colors, My World. Mis Colores, Mi Mundo*. San Francisco: Children's Book Press, 2007.
A young girl introduces the colors of the desert. In English and Spanish.

Horáček, Petr. *Butterfly, Butterfly*. Cambridge, MA: Candlewick Press, 2007.
A little girl follows a butterfly in the garden. Clever cutouts and a surprise at the end.

Jones, Christianne, C. *Big Red Farm*. Minneapolis, MN: Picture Window Books, 2007.
Learn about colors and mixing colors to make new colors. See others in this series, <u>Know</u> <u>Your Colors</u>.

Kann, Victoria. *Pinkalicious*. New York: HarperCollins, 2006.

Kann, Victoria. *Purplicious*. New York: HarperCollins, 2007.
The colors pink and purple are delicious.

Kochalka, James. *Squirrelly Gray*.
The adventure begins when a squirrel who lives in a colorless world loses his two front teeth and meets the tooth fairy

Lopshire, Robert. *Put Me in the Zoo*. New York: Beginner Books; distributed by Random House, 1960.
  Colors, spots, stripes: you name it!

Marks, Jennifer L. *Sorting by Color*. Mankato, MN: Capstone Press, 2007.
  Clear and colorful pictures of everyday objects. Good vocabulary builder.

Martin, Bill. *Brown Bear, Brown Bear, What do You See?* New York: Henry Holt, 1983.
  A wonderful refrain, colors, and animals. Also in Spanish: *Oso Pardo, Oso Pardo, Que Ves Ahi?*. Translated by Teresa Mlawer.

Rusch, Elizabeth. *A Day with No Crayons*. Flagstaff, AZ: Rising Moon, 2007.
  A little girl creates art during a day with no crayons.

Seeger, Laura Vaccaro. *Lemons Are Not Red*. Brookfield, CT: Roaring Brook Press, 2004.
  Each page contains a cutout of a familiar shape, and the color it is not—until you turn the page.

Slater, Dashka. *Baby Shoes*. New York: Bloomsbury Children's; distributed to the trade by Holtzbrinck Publishers, 2006.
  Written in rhyming verse. Baby's new shoes soon become multicolored as he stomps through the park.

Williams, Sue. *I Went Walking*. San Diego: Harcourt Brace Jovanovich, 1990.
  A boy meets animals of different colors while on a walk. Also in Spanish: *Salí de Paseo*. Translated by Alma F. Ada.

Homonyms and Homophones

Words that sound alike but mean different things are the focus of the following booklist. Caregivers may use the pictures in the books to talk with their children about words that sound the same but have different meanings. Booklist from "Piggy Rae and the Blue Ribbon Blues."

Alda, Arlene. *Did You Say Pears?* Toronto: Tundra Books, 2006.
  Stunning photographs pair homophonic words and phrases.

Barretta, Gene. *Dear Deer: A Book of Homophones*. New York: Henry Holt, 2007.
  Aunt Ant writes a Dear Deer letter from the zoo.

Cazet, Denys. *Will You Read to Me?* New York: Atheneum Books for Young Readers, 2007.
  A cute story about a pig who likes poetry more than mud.

Cleary, Brian P. *How Much Can a Bare Bear Bear?: What Are Homonyms and Homophones?* Minneapolis, MN: Millbrook Press, 2005.
  Rhyming text introduces homonyms and homophones.

Couric, Katie. *The Blue Ribbon Day*. New York: Doubleday, 2004.
  Not about homonyms, but helps explain blue ribbons in greater detail.

Feiffer, Kate. *Henry, the Dog with No Tail*. New York: Simon & Schuster, 2007
  Clever self-esteem story that also features a play on words.

Gwynne, Fred. *A Chocolate Moose for Dinner*. New York: Windmill Books, 1976
  Well-illustrated book about popular phrases that can seem to have two meanings.

Hambleton, Laura. *Telling Tails: Fun with Homonyms*. Chicago: Milet Publishing, LLC, 2006.
Fun! Silly pictures and text.

Howe, James. *Horace and Morris But Mostly Dolores*. New York: Atheneum Books for Young
Readers, 1997.
Makes vocabulary word play around various references to cheese.

Kasza, Keiko. *Badger's Fancy Meal*. New York: G. P. Putnam's Sons, 2007
This badger badgers.

O'Malley, Kevin. *Gimme Cracked Corn and I Will Share*. New York: Walker; distributed to the
trade by Holtzbrinck Publishers, 2007.
Every pun imaginable is used here. Very funny.

Thomas, Shelley Moore. *Take Care, Good Knight*. New York: Dutton Children's Books, 2006.
Dragons try to interpret a wizard's message, which has double meanings.

Walsh, Vivian. *Olive, the Other Reindeer*. San Francisco: Chronicle Books, 1997.
Olive the dog thinks this popular song is written about her. Is she a dog or a reindeer?

West, Colin. *Buzz, Buzz, Buzz Went Bumblebee*. Cambridge, MA: Candlewick Press, 1996.
A bumblebee buzzes around all day, until he finds someone who doesn't tell him to "buzz
off!"

Ziefert, Harriet. *Night, Knight*. Boston: Houghton Mifflin, 1997
A lift-the-flap word comparative.

"Write On!" (series). Edina, MN: ABDO Publishing, 2002– .

Doudna, Kelly. *An Ear Is Not an Ear*. 2002

Rondeau, Amanda. *The Prince Left His Prints*. 2002.

Scheunemann, Pam. *Sam Has a Sundae on Sunday*. 2002.

Building Vocabulary

These books contain descriptive words and phrases. They are useful for introducing new nouns and
adjectives. Booklist from "Cautious Tommy Turtle."

Brett, Jan. *The Mitten: A Ukrainian Folktale*. New York: Putnam, 1989.
Name the animals who manage to squeeze into a knitted white mitten.

Cronin, Doreen. *Click, Clack, Moo: Cows that Type*. New York: Simon & Schuster Books for
Young Readers, 2000.
The cows type letters to the farmer demanding better living conditions. Descriptive phrases.

Ehlert, Lois. *Snowballs*. San Diego: Harcourt Brace, 1995.
Names the items used to build snowmen, then describes them.

Elting, Mary. *Q Is for Duck: An Alphabet Guessing Game*. New York: Houghton
Mifflin/Clarion Books, c1980, 2005.
Q is for duck because a duck says "quack," and other unconventional alphabet riddles.
Good vocabulary guessing game.

Emmett, Jonathan. *Through the Heart of the Jungle*. Wilton, CT: Tiger Tales, 2003.
> A cumulative rhyme along the lines of "I Know an Old Lady Who Swallowed a Fly." Focuses on different words for eating.

Hindley, Judy. *Baby Talk: A Book of First Words and Phrases*. Cambridge, MA: Candlewick Press, 2006.
> The words a baby uses while talking about his day.

Johnson, David. *Snow Sounds: An Onomatopoeic Story*. Boston: Houghton Mifflin, 2006.
> *Crunch, jingly, scrape*—words that describe a snowy wonderland.

Menchin, Scott. *Taking a Bath with the Dog and Other Things That Make Me Happy*. Cambridge, MA: Candlewick Press, 2007.
> Various people describe what makes them happy.

Meyers, Susan. *Kittens! Kittens! Kittens!* New York: Abrams Books for Young Readers, 2007.
> Adjectives that describe the life of pouncing, bouncing kittens.

Moss, Miriam. *Bare Bear*. New York: Holiday House, 2005.
> A bare bear looks everywhere for a missing striped sock.

O'Connor, Jane. *Fancy Nancy*. New York: HarperCollins, 2005.

O'Connor, Jane. *Fancy Nancy and the Posh Puppy*. New York: HarperCollins, 2007.

O'Connor, Jane. *Fancy Nancy's Favorite Fancy Words: From Accessories to Zany*. New York: HarperCollins, 2008.
> This series distinguishes itself by using fancy words.

Prince, April Jones. *What Do Wheels Do All Day?* Boston: Houghton Mifflin, 2006.
> Names objects with wheels.

Rosen, Michael. *We're Going on a Bear Hunt*. New York: Margaret K. McElderry Books, 1989.
> Going on a bear hunt, and along the way they climb a grassy slope, swish across a river, and sludge through the mud.

Scieszka, Jon. *The Stinky Cheese Man and Other Fairly Stupid Tales*. New York: Viking, 1992.
> Funny stories, loaded with descriptive words.

Shore, Diane Z. *Look Both Ways: A Cautionary Tale*. New York: Bloomsbury Children's Books, 2005
> Words of warning to a squirrel who forgets to look before crossing the street.

Sperring, Mark. *Mermaid Dreams*. New York: Scholastic, 2006.
> Descriptive beach and ocean words in a sweet mermaid story.

Tafuri, Nancy. *The Busy Little Squirrel*. New York: Simon & Schuster Books for Young Readers, c2007.
> Squirrel is busy—he has no time to nibble, hop, or run.

The 20th Century Children's Book Treasury. New York: Knopf; distributed by Random House, 1998.
> Contains a wealth of exceptional children's literature. Also great to read through for other literacy skill ideas.

Viorst, Judith. *Absolutely Positively Alexander: Alexander the Complete Stories*. New York: Atheneum Books for Young Readers, c1972, 1978, 1995, 1997.
> Contains the Alexander stories, including *Alexander and the Terrible, Horrible, No Good, Very Bad Day*.

Wood, Audrey. *The Napping House* San Diego: Harcourt Brace Jovanovich, 1984.
> A quiet household until the wakeful flea comes along.

Yolen, Jane. *Sleep, Black Bear, Sleep*. New York: HarperCollins Children's Books, 2007.
> Sleepful, nodding, resting animals cozy up inside their homes while it snows outside.

Building Vocabulary with Useful Descriptive Words and Phrases

Caregivers can reinforce language development by using some of these descriptive words when talking to their children. Booklist from "Mrs. Know-It-All Game Show: Mind Your Manners."

Beaumont, Karen. *I Ain't Gonna Paint No More*. Orlando, FL: Harcourt, 2005.
> Focuses on names of colors, body parts, and rhyme.

Dewdney, Anna. *Llama, Llama Mad at Mama*. New York: Viking, 2007.
> Descriptive adjectives are used to describe this shopping adventure. Includes a lesson on using proper manners.

Dunbar, Joyce. *Shoe Baby*. Cambridge, MA: Candlewick Press, 2005.
> Shoe baby goes places with a very kind, "How do you do?"

Gliori, Debi. *Flora's Blanket*. New York: Orchard Books, 2001.
> Flora's blanket is missing, and the family is looking for it. Names rooms in the house and common objects.

Hindley, Judy. *Baby Talk: A Book of First Words and Phrases*. Cambridge, MA: Candlewick Press, 2006.
> Names locations, both indoors and out, and some first words that revolve around baby's day.

Jenkins, Steve. *Move!* Boston: Houghton Mifflin, 2006.
> Animal movement words—*leap, run, crawl*.

Katz, Alan. *Are You Quite Polite? Silly Dilly Manners Songs*. New York: Margaret K. McElderry Books, 2006.
> Funny songs, new vocabulary; kids will love this.

Levin, Bridget. *Rules of the Wild: An Unruly Book of Manners*. San Francisco: Chronicle Books, 2004.
> Defines good manners for animals and good manners for people.

Rosenthal, Amy Krouse. *Cookies: Bite-size Life Lessons*. New York: HarperCollins, 2006.
> Uses examples with cookies, to describe sharing and other good manners.

Sierra, Judy. *Mind Your Manners, B. B. Wolf*. New York: Knopf, 2007.
> The Big Bad Wolf behaves himself in the retirement village.

Spinelli, Eileen. *When You Are Happy*. New York: Simon & Schuster Books for Young Readers, 2006.

> Builds vocabulary by talking about feelings.

Weatherford, Carole Boston. *Jazz Baby*. New York: Lee & Low Books, 2002.

> Vocabulary introduced is names of musical instruments.

Wells, Rosemary. *Yoko's World of Kindness: Golden Rules for a Happy Classroom*. New York: Hyperion Books, 2005.

> Getting along with others, teasing, and separation anxiety are presented in six short stories, along with reinforcing vocabulary development.

Letter Knowledge

Focus on the Letter *B*

The letter *B* is featured frequently in the text and/or titles of these engaging read-alouds. Booklist from "Bernie Bear's Birthday."

Anderson, Derek. *Gladys Goes Out to Lunch*. New York: Simon & Schuster Books for Young Readers, 2005.

> Gladys is a gorilla who spices up her diet by discovering banana bread.

Bruss, Deborah. *Book! Book! Book!* New York: Scholastic, 2001.

> Farm animals discover the joy of reading. Hens don't cluck, they say, "Book! Book! Book!"

McPhail, David. *Big Brown Bear's Birthday Surprise*. Orlando, FL: Harcourt, 2007.

> A big brown bear's friend, Rat, is giving him a birthday present that has four letters and starts with a *B*.

Mitton, Tony. *Busy Boats*. New York: Kingfisher, 2002

> All kinds of boats and what they are used for.

Patricelli, Leslie. *The Birthday Box*. Cambridge, MA: Candlewick Press, 2007.

> An imaginative child finds many uses for a box.

Building Letter Knowledge

All letters of the alphabet are effectively introduced in the following books.
Booklist from "Bernie Bear's Birthday."

Blackstone, Stella. *Cleo's Alphabet Book*. Cambridge, MA: Barefoot Books, 2003.

> Clues are given for readers to guess the object described.

Cleary, Brian P. *Peanut Butter and Jellyfishes: A Very Silly Alphabet Book*. Minneapolis, MN: Millbrook Press, 2007.

> Search the pages to find the alphabet letters, words that start with the letters, and silly rhymes.

Delessert, Etienne. *Aa: A was an Apple Pie, an English Nursery Rhyme*. Mankato, MN: Creative Editions, 2005.

> Clear text and pictures make this book a winner.

Dog Artlist Collection (Firm). *The Dog From Arf! Arf! to Zzzzzz.* New York: HarperCollins, 2004.

> The reader may not intuitively know the letter of the alphabet being represented, but dog lovers will want to examine this book.

Lobel, Anita. *Animal Antics: A to Z.* New York: Greenwillow Books, 2005.

> Animals, animal sounds, and letters in one fun book.

MacDonald, Ross. *Achoo! Bang! Crash!: A Noisy Alphabet.* Brookfield, CT: Roaring Brook Press, 2003.

> An interactive alphabet book; make sounds while learning letters.

Marino, Gianna. *Zoopa: An Alphabet Soup ABC.* San Francisco: Chronicle Books, 2005.

> A simple bowl of tomato soup evolves as each page introduces another animal and its antics.

Meddaugh, Susan. *Martha Speaks.* Boston: Houghton Mifflin, 1992.

> Not an alphabet book, but this talking dog offers an excellent way to bring attention to letters of the alphabet.

O'Keefe, Susan Heyboer. *Hungry Monster ABC.* New York: Little, Brown, 2007.

> Wonderful and funny illustrations with loveable monsters.

Pallotta, Jerry. *The Construction Alphabet Book.* Watertown, MA: Charlesbridge, 2006.

> Construction vehicles, from the well known to the little known.

Pearson, Debora. *Alphabeep: A Zipping, Zooming ABC.* New York: Holiday House, 2003.

> Vehicles from ambulance to zamboni, with the sounds to go along with them.

Wallace, Nancy Elizabeth. *Alphabet House.* New York: Marshall Cavendish, 2005.

> Connects objects found in everyday life with their first letter. Colors also.

Narrative Skills

Reading these "Cinderella" stories from around the world will present opportunities for storytelling. Suggest that caregivers embellish upon the segment of the "Cinderella" story told in the puppet show. The second list contains other recommended children's literature that offers opportunities for reading and retelling. Booklist from "Moosterpiece Theater: Piggy Rae-ella."

Building Narrative Skills: "Cinderella" Stories from Around the World

Climo, Shirley. *The Korean Cinderella.* New York: HarperCollins, 1993.

> Delight in the accomplishments of Pear Blossom.

Compton, Joanne Ward. *Ashpet, an Appalachian Tale.* New York: Holiday House, 1994.

> Instead of a fancy dress ball, this "Cinderella" story takes place at a "church meetin'," and the handsome prince is the doctor's son.

Craft, K. Y. *Cinderella.* New York: SeaStar Books, 2000.

> Lavish illustrations reminiscent of seventeenth-century French art.

dePaola, Tomie. *Adelita: A Mexican Cinderella Story.* New York: G.P. Putnam's Sons, 2002.

> This story uses some Spanish text that is translated within the work.

Ehrlich, Amy. *Cinderella.* By Charles Perrault; adapted by Amy Ehrlich. New York: Dutton Children's Books, 1985.

> Renowned for its beautiful illustrations by Susan Jeffers.

Fleischman, Paul. *Glass Slipper, Gold Sandal: A Worldwide Cinderella.* New York: Henry Holt, 2007.

> Combines multiple cultural retellings of "Cinderella" into one story.

Goode, Diane. *Cinderella, the Dog and Her Little Glass Slipper.* New York: Blue Sky Press, 2000.

> This version has dogs instead of people.

Hayes, Joe. *Little Gold Star: A Cinderella Story. Estrellita de Oro: a Cinderella Cuento.* El Paso, TX: Cinco Pontos Press, 2000.

> Retold in Spanish and English. A bright gold star glows brightly on Arcía's forehead and attracts the attention of the prince.

Hickox, Rebecca. *The Golden Sandal: A Middle Eastern Cinderella.* New York: Holiday House, 1998.

> A magical fish and a delicate gold sandal are part of this Middle Eastern version of "Cinderella."

Hill, Margaret Bateson. *Chanda and the Mirror of Moonlight.* Chicago: Zero To Ten, 2001.

> The story takes place in India and is written in both English and Hindi.

Marineau, Michèle. *Cinderella.* Toronto: Tundra Books, 2007.

> This modern interpretation of "Cinderella" features a gal who takes charge of her own life and goes to the ball in a sports car and pointy-toed shoes.

Perlman, Janet. *Cinderella Penguin: or, The Little Glass Flipper.* New York: Viking: Puffin Books, 1992.

> A delightful variation, with penguins.

San Souci, Daniel. *Sootface: An Ojibwa Cinderella Story.* New York: Doubleday Book for Young Readers, 1994.

> An Ojibwa tale, very similar to *The Rough-Face Girl* by Rafe Martin.

Young, Amy. *Belinda and the Glass Slipper.* New York: Viking, 2006.

> This version is for ballet lovers.

Other Stories to Read and Retell

Denise, Anika. *Pigs Love Potatoes.* New York: Philomel Books, 2007.

> A counting and rhyming book. Try to remember who stopped by mama's house wanting to eat potatoes.

Ehrlich, Amy. *The Random House Book of Fairy Tales.* New York: Random House, 1985.

> A collection of much-loved fairy tales.

Garland, Michael. *How Many Mice?* New York: Dutton Children's Books, 2007.

> Succinct sentences advance the plot. Also introduces numbers and math.

Inches, Alison. *The Stuffed Animals Get Ready for Bed.* Orlando, FL: Harcourt, 2006.

> A little girl patiently prepares her naughty stuffed animals for bedtime.

Krensky, Stephen. *Big Bad Wolves at School*. New York: Simon & Schuster Books for Young Readers, 2007.

    A nature-loving wolf goes to big bad wolf school to learn to huff and puff.

LaRochelle, David. *The End*. New York: Arthur A. Levine Books, 2006.

    This fairy tale told in reverse—it begins with, "They lived happily ever after." An innovative storytelling technique.

Lester, Helen. *Tacky the Penguin*. Boston: Houghton Mifflin, 1988.

    A penguin who has his own way of doing things saves his friends.

Murphy, Jill. *Mr. Large in Charge*. Cambridge, MA: Candlewick Press, 2007.

    When Mrs. Large, an elephant, has to spend the day sick in bed, Mr. Large takes over running the household.

Ohi, Ruth. *Me and My Brother*. Toronto: Annick Press, 2007.

    Story of two brothers and how they play.

Plourde, Lynn. *A Mountain of Mittens*. Watertown, MA: Charlesbridge, 2007.

    After reading this book, try to remember how many ways the main character lost her mittens.

Shulman, Lisa. *Over in the Meadow at the Big Ballet*. New York: Putnam, 2007.

    Review all the steps necessary to put on a dance recital.

Thompson, Lauren. *Little Quack*. New York: Simon & Schuster Books for Young Readers, 2003.

    A hesitant duck gets ready for a swim.

Weninger, Brigitte. *Bye-bye, Binky*. New York: Minedition/Penguin Young Readers Group, 2007.

    You'll enjoy talking about this story of a kitten who is ready to give up her pacifier.

Index

ABOUT THE AUTHOR

Laurel L. Iakovakis was a children's librarian and the District Youth Collection Development Librarian at Douglas County Libraries, Castle Rock, Colorado. She is currently employed by the Richardson Public Library, Richardson, Texas, where she works in the youth services department and provides outreach and storytime services.